"THIS PRACTICE AGAINST LAW"

CUBAN SLAVE TRADE CASES *in the* SOUTHERN DISTRICT *of* NEW YORK, 1839-1841

JOHN D. GORDAN, III

Samuel Rossiter Betts

"THIS PRACTICE AGAINST LAW"

CUBAN SLAVE TRADE CASES *in the* SOUTHERN DISTRICT *of* NEW YORK, 1839-1841

JOHN D. GORDAN, III

TALBOT PUBLISHING
Clark, New Jersey

ISBN 978-1-61619-545-8

TALBOT PUBLISHING
AN IMPRINT OF
THE LAWBOOK EXCHANGE, LTD.
33 Terminal Avenue
Clark, New Jersey 07066-1321

Please see our website for a selection of our other publications and fine facsimile reprints of classic works of legal history:
www.lawbookexchange.com

Library of Congress Cataloging-in-Publication Data

Names: Gordan, John D., 1945- author.
Title: "This practice against law" : Cuban slave trade cases in the Southern District of New York, 1839-1841 / by John D. Gordan, III.
Description: Clark, NJ : Talbot Publishing An Imprint of The Lawbook Exchange, Ltd., 2016. | Includes bibliographical references and index.
Identifiers: LCCN 2016041164 | ISBN 9781616195458 (hardcover : alk. paper)
Subjects: LCSH: Catharine (Ship)--Trials, litigation, etc. | Butterfly (Ship)--Trials, litigation, etc. | United States. District Court (New York : Southern District) | Slaves--Legal status, laws, etc.--New York (State)--History--19th century. | Slavery--New York (State)--Legal status of slaves in free states. | Slavery--Law and legislation--New York (State)--History--19th century. | Slave trade--United States--History--19th century. | Slave trade--Cuba--History--19th century. | Slave trade--Cuba--Cases. | Slave ships--United States--History--19th century.
Classification: LCC KF228.C33 G67 2016 | DDC 345.73/02551--dc23
LC record available at https://lccn.loc.gov/2016041164

Printed in the United States of America on acid-free paper

FOR KITTY,
ELIZABETH AND JOHN

ACKNOWLEDGMENTS

This little book is an effort to clarify a misunderstood moment—distorted by its context of depravity and human suffering—in the history of a court which is first in several ways: the United States district court for the southern district of New York. It could not have reached the press without the insights and encouragement of my constant editor and friend, Conrad K. Harper, and of my two readers and friends, Judge Morris Sheppard Arnold and Judge Jed S. Rakoff, for which I am ever grateful. I would also like to thank the past and present employees of the National Archives and Records Administration, New York Branch, who invariably provided me with prompt and professional assistance during the preparation of this book.

I am also indebted to Greg Talbot of Talbot Publishing Co. for his willingness to publish a second book of mine and for giving me another opportunity to have the pleasure of working with his colleague, Valerie Horowitz.

I find, then, as a matter of fact, that in the month of June, 1839, the law of Spain did prohibit, under severe penalty, the importation into Cuba of negroes from Africa.... Why did they not ascertain that the law of Spain had declared these objects of their purchase not slaves? The secret is told in a word. In Cuba it is the custom to buy such negroes...; and there respectable men have grown up under the influence of this custom—*this practice against law*.

Gedney v. L'Amistad, 10 Fed. Cas. 141, 146–147
(Case No. 5294a) (D. Conn. 1840)

TABLE OF CONTENTS

INTRODUCTION

The "Legal History" section of the 1963 *Annual Survey of American Law*, written by the future dean of legal historians, John Phillip Reid, contains a laudatory paragraph about a book published by the University of California Press that year, entitled *American Slavers and the Federal Law, 1837–1864,* by Warren S. Howard:

> "Revisionism" is the chief historiographic theme to emerge from this survey year. Knocking Whig historians remains good sport on both sides of the Atlantic. An especially fine reappraisal has been turned in by Warren S. Howard, historian at Vandenberg Air Force Base. He challenges the traditional assumption that the debacle in enforcement of the anti-slave trade laws was engineered by Southern slaveowners who paralyzed effective police action through their control of the national administration. Familiar villains such as Buchanan are exonerated, and blame is shifted to legal technicalities and to disinterested minor officials—particularly judges in the Southern District of New York. His evidence is convincing....[1]

American Slavers covers an extensive array of cases and does give every indication of familiarity in depth with their legal records; it is without doubt the best available source for a review of the cases it addresses,

---

[1] 681, 682 (footnotes omitted). The book was an extension of Howard's Ph.D. thesis. No additional writing by the author on this or related subjects has been identified.

and is recognized as such. As Professor Reid said, it places responsibility for unacceptable outcomes on judges sitting in the southern district of New York and lays on them some of the blame for the persistence of the international slave trade.

This book considers the proceedings held in connection with just two of the earliest slave ship cases Howard discusses—the *Butterfly* and the *Catharine*—seized with their crews by the British Navy off the coast of Africa within a two-week period in August 1839 and sailed with prize crews to the southern district of New York for forfeiture proceedings. These cases differ from others because the ships involved were then American in name only: the ships were built for the slave trade in Baltimore and flying the American flag, to be sure, but the ventures they set out on were organized in Havana, their point of departure for Africa and the intended destination of their human cargo.

Howard identifies aspects of those nearly unique cases as evidence supporting his criticism, but a comprehensive consideration of the circumstances of those cases as a whole, in their jurisprudential context, leads to a different conclusion. The response of the federal judiciary, both in the southern district of New York and related cases in the district of Maryland, to the unexpected appearance of those vessels here reflects well on the judges, and, perhaps surprisingly, best on Chief Justice Roger Brooke Taney, sitting as a Circuit Justice in Baltimore and presiding in the Supreme Court of the United States. The two instances of judicial hesitancy in the southern district of New York were both consistent with settled legal principles and had no effect on the final outcome.

The task facing the New York federal judges in these two cases was in many ways novel and made the harder by a number of external factors. First, those involved in the voyages of the *Butterfly* and particularly the *Catharine* were experienced in the Cuban slave trade and, in the case of the latter, the leaders of their profession; they were responsive to the rhythms of international anti-slavery enforcement, and the elaborate ruse of back-to-back sales of the vessel, a dummy charter and shifting national flags which they adopted to thwart it purposefully created the confusion in the initial proceedings in the district court against the *Catharine*.

Second, the New York district court was here constrained by the evidentiary limitations of 19th century prize courts,[2] and its distance from British authorities on the West coast of Africa, who were aggressive and stalwart in enforcing their nation's opposition to the international slave traffic, prevented the presentation of the evidence they had collected of the extensive involvement in the Cuban slave trade of some of the individuals openly participating in the supposedly innocent voyages of these two ships. However, some evidence had been previously passed on to the American government by the British Foreign Minister, Lord Palmerston, and the U.S. Consul in Havana. More of it was available in the records of a related case against the builders of the *Catharine* in the United States circuit court in Baltimore and of the case involving the slave ship *Amistad* in the district court in Connecticut, all under way at the same time. There is no indication in the record that any of this information was ever presented to Samuel Rossiter Betts, the district judge in the southern district of New York before whom the *Butterfly* and the *Catharine* first came.

---

[2] Samuel Rossiter Betts, *A Summary of Practice in Instance, Revenue and Prize Causes in the Admiralty Courts of the United States for the Southern District of New-York; and also on Appeal to the Supreme Court; Together with the Rules of the District Court* (New York: Halstead and Voorhies 1838), 72-73; [James Stephen], *War in Disguise; or the Frauds of the Neutral Flags.* (London Printed: New-York: I. Riley January, 1806) 96, 178–179.

PART I

CONTEXT

CHAPTER 1

The International Slave Trade

Following its prohibition of British involvement in the international slave trade in 1807, Great Britain set out to terminate that trade through numerous bilateral treaties, made, among others, with the principal participants in the trade, Spain and Portugal. Each of those countries signed treaties in 1817, Portugal's supplementing an earlier declaration of 1810 and a treaty of 1815, granting Great Britain the right to search suspected slave ships flying its flag but to seize only those with slaves then on board for adjudication by Courts of Mixed Commission. These were courts established locally under each treaty, staffed with one judge appointed by each of the parties to the treaty and one arbitrator similarly appointed and added by lot to the adjudication of any particular case if the two judges failed to agree. However, these treaties had other limitations: Spain's only took effect north of the Equator when signed and south of the Equator in 1820; Portugal's only applied north of the Equator and was limited to fifteen years.[3]

---

[3] Arthur F. Corwin, *Spain and the Abolition of Slavery in Cuba, 1817–1886* (Austin: Univ. of Texas Press 2014; paperback edition), 28–30; Leslie Bethell, *The Abolition of the Brazilian Slave Trade: Britain, Brazil and the Slave Trade Question 1807–1869* (Cambridge 1970), 18–21; David R. Murray, *Odious commerce: Britain, Spain and the abolition of the Cuban slave trade* (Cambridge 1980), 67–70; Jenny S. Martinez, *The Slave Trade and the Origins of International Human Rights Law* (Oxford 2012), 31–36, 67–70, 78–79; David

Constrained by the opposition of their principal colonies, Cuba and Brazil, neither Spain nor Portugal made any efforts to curtail the international slave trade themselves,[4] leaving to Great Britain the enforcement of the treaties at sea.[5] The Duke of Wellington, then Foreign Secretary, characterized the slave trade to Cuba in early 1835 thus:

> The prevalence of that trade, the impunity with which it is carried on, the absence of any real inquiry into the Cases, notwithstanding continual remonstrances to the Local Authorities from His Majesty's Commissioners, notwithstanding also repetitions of remonstrances upon the same subject from His Majesty's Government to that of Spain, all conspire to denote that the Local Government of Cuba protects this detestable Trade under the positive Instructions of the Spanish Government at home.[6]

If observed, the restriction of seizures to vessels actually carrying slaves when boarded hampered British enforcement efforts. In June 1835 Great Britain and Spain entered into a new treaty with a so-called "Equip-

---

Turnbull, *Travels in the West. Cuba: with Notices of Porto Rico, and the Slave Trade* (London: Longman 1840), 384–389; J. P. van Niekerk, "British, Portuguese, and American Judges in Adderley Street: the international legal background to and some judicial aspects of the Cape Town Mixed Commissions for the suppression of the transatlantic slave trade in the nineteen century (Part 1)," 37 (2004) *Comp. and Int'l. Law Journal of South Africa* 1.

[4] Murray, 128–132. "In one of the ironies of history, the destruction of slavery in Saint-Domingue gave an immense stimulus to plantation slavery from neighboring Cuba to far-off Brazil." David Brion Davis, *The Problem of Slavery in the Age of Emancipation* (New York: Knopf 2014), 47–48.

[5] Murray, 77.

[6] *British and Foreign State Papers, 1835–1836,* 24 (London: Ridgway 1853), 178 (The Duke of Wellington to George Villiers, British Ambassador to Spain, February 27, 1835).

ment Clause", allowing the seizure and condemnation of vessels plainly equipped for the slave trade but not carrying slaves at the time of search.[7] Negotiations to obtain a similar concession from Portugal were unsuccessfully carried on for years with rising British annoyance, and on August 24, 1839, Parliament passed a statute unilaterally authorizing the British Navy to search and seize any Portuguese vessel carrying slaves or equipped to do so and to send the vessel to British vice-admiralty courts for prize adjudication. In 1845 it passed a similar statute applicable to Brazilian vessels.[8]

Despite its own domestic prohibitions of the importation of slaves, the United States repeatedly rebuffed British

---

[7] Murray, 100–101; Corwin, 61–62.

[8] Bethell, 155–164. "The second act, passed in 1845 and often called Lord Aberdeen's Act, was virtually identical to its predecessor except that it was directed against ships sailing under the Brazilian flag and was marginally less offensive in international law. Most of the Anglo-Brazilian slave-trade treaty of 1826 was of indefinite duration. However, that part of it that provided for mutual right of search and created the Anglo-Brazilian courts of mixed commission was based on the 1817 Anglo-Portuguese convention, that had a twenty-eight-year term. From March 1845 British cruisers would not be able to interfere with Brazilian slave ships. Moreover, even with the right of search in force there had always been considerable doubt as to whether the mixed courts could condemn Brazilian slave ships with no slaves on board. An additional article covering these cases had been signed by Brazil and Britain in July 1835, but the former had never ratified it. ... Brazilian reluctance to renew the right-of-search clause and to ratify the equipment article induced Aberdeen to duplicate the measure already in use against Portugal. Because the first article of the 1826 treaty declared the trade to be piracy for British and Brazilian subjects and was subject to no time constraint, the British were able to claim that the act merely enforced existing treaty provisions." But Aberdeen admitted that the act was "a great stretch of power" and open to many objections. David Eltis, *Economic Growth and the Ending of the Transatlantic Slave Trade* (New York: Oxford University Press 1987, paperback edition 1989), 89–90 (footnotes omitted).

overtures to enter into a similar treaty to interdict participation in the international slave trade by American vessels. The British Navy's search and seizure of neutral American ships during the Napoleonic Wars in the minds of many was the underlying cause for the War of 1812. Secretary of State John Quincy Adams asserted that Constitutional constraints on the adjudication of American rights by Courts of Mixed Commission precluded such an agreement.[9] An effort to forge a collaboration between the United States and Great Britain, endorsed by the House of Representatives and Adams in 1823, was amended to death in the Senate because of the British insistence on the right to search U.S. ships.[10] Informal cooperation between the two countries' naval forces off the African coast in the early 1840 was promptly repudiated in Washington.[11]

---

[9] Eugene Kontorovich, "The Constitutionality of International Courts – The Forgotten Precedent of Slave-Trade Tribunals", 158 (2009) *U. Pa. L. Rev.* 39, 58–74; *ibid.,* "Three International Courts and Their Constitutional Problems," 99 (2014) *Cornell L. Rev.* 1353.

[10] As Martin Van Buren put it:

> The measure now referred to was the concession to Great Britain by treaty stipulation of the Right of Search to prevent the prosecution of the slave trade under our flag, a pretension against which, when attempted to be put into practice for the purpose of recovering British seamen from our service, we had waged a war – the cause of which was yet fresh in the recollection of the People, as well as the irritations produced by it. We opposed the treaty and defeated it by a decided vote.

Autobiography of Martin Van Buren (Ann. Report of the Am. Hist. Soc., Washington, D.C., U.S. Gov. Printing Office, 2 Vols., 1920) II, 203. Worthington Chauncey Ford (ed.), *The Papers of John Quincy Adams* (New York: Macmillan 1917), VII, 489–516; Don E. Fehrenbacher, *The Slaveholding Republic: An Account of the United States Government's Relations to Slavery* (Oxford 2001), 152–160; Bethell, 24–25; Seymour Drescher, *A History of Slavery and Antislavery* (Cambridge 2009), 312.

[11] Martinez, 86–87; Bethell 191.

David Turnbull, British consul in Havana until he was expelled and a tireless abolitionist agitator, proposed that Parliament enact a statute granting the British Navy the same powers against United States vessels as its 1839 law concerning Portugal.[12]

In December, 1841, despite the demonstration by these and other cases of the inadequacy of existing treaty arrangements in combating the international slave trade, President Tyler still told Congress that:

> I herewith submit the correspondence which has recently taken place between the American minister at the Court of St. James, Mr. Stevenson, and the Minister of Foreign Affairs of that Government on the right claimed by that Government to visit and detain vessels sailing under the American flag, and engaged in prosecuting lawful commerce in the African seas.... However desirous the United States may be for the suppression of the slave trade, they cannot consent to interpolations into the maritime code, at the mere will and pleasure of other governments.... We claim to have a voice in all amendments or alterations of that code – and when we are given to understand, as in this instance, by a foreign Government, that its treaties with other nations cannot be executed without the establishment and enforcement of new principles of maritime police, to be applied without our consent, we must employ a language neither of equivocal import, nor susceptible of misconstruction. American citizens prosecuting a lawful commerce in the African seas, under the flag of their country, are not responsible for the abuse or unlawful use of that flag by others; nor can they rightfully on account of such

---

[12] Turnbull, 379–381.

> alleged abuses, be interrupted, molested or detained while in the ocean....[13]

In early 1842, relying on the President's message, Lewis Cass, the United States Ambassador to France and a Presidential aspirant, successfully importuned the French government to refuse to execute the so-called "Quintuple Treaty" organized by Great Britain to facilitate effective suppression to the international slave trade. Justifying the refusal of the United States to participate in a treaty arrangement involving the right of mutual search, Cass issued an anonymous pamphlet:

> No, it is not African slavery, the United-States wish to encourage. It is, as we shall see, by and by, American slavery, the slavery of American sailors, they seek to prevent.[14]

Benefiting from American recalcitrance and in an effort to avoid expanded enforcement by the British Navy empowered by the 1835 treaty with Spain, slave traders turned to swift clipper ships built in Baltimore and flew Portuguese and, increasingly, American flags on their vessels, the latter particularly on outbound voyages to Africa.[15] At the time, the Mixed Commission in Sierra

---

[13] Message of the President, Cong. Globe, 27th Cong., 2d Sess., December, 1841, App. 1–2.

[14] An American [Lewis Cass], *An Examination of the Question, Now in Discussion, Between American and British Governments, Concerning the Right of Search* (N.P, N.D.) [Paris, 1842], 13. See also "Gen. Cass and the Quintuple Treaty" ("Published under Authority of the National and Jackson Democratic Association Committee", N.D.[1848])

[15] Corwin, 62–63; Bethell, 186–191; Turnbull, 154.

Leone refused to assert jurisdiction over vessels flying the American flag seized by the British Navy.[16]

Driven by "the universal belief in Cuba that without African slave labour the island's wealth would be destroyed," the planters in Cuba successfully insisted on the importation of an ever-increasing number of slaves for their expanding sugar crops with the connivance and financial participation of local officials in Havana: Captain-General Tacon in Havana and even the Queen are said to have been paid bribes based on the number of slaves imported.[17] The British commissioners, stationed in Havana under Great Britain's treaty with Spain but with no cases to adjudicate there, insisted that the American Consul, Nicholas P. Trist, aided and abetted the slave traders.[18]

---

[16] *The Trial of Pedro De Zulueta, Jun., on a Charge of Slave Trading* (London, C. Wood & Co. 1844), 10–11.

[17] Robin Blackburn, *The American Crucible: Slavery, Emancipation and Human Rights* (New York: Verso 2011), 287–288, 293–294; Murray, 76–77, 89; Corwin, 50, 55, 59. Edward J. Mullen (ed.), *The Life and Poems of a Cuban Slave: Juan Francisco Manzano 1797–1854* (New York: Palgrave MacMillan 2014), 121–122, reproduces a dialogue attributed to Richard R. Madden and an unidentified Cuban which states that in his four years as Captain-General in the 1830s, Tacon received $450,000 in this way.

[18] Turnbull, 435–450. Further discussion of Trist's activities in Havana appears *infra* at pp. 60–64, but a brief introduction to this extraordinary individual would not be premature. Trist was a Virginian and married Thomas Jefferson's eldest granddaughter; he drew Jefferson's will, was with him when he died, and administered his estate. James Madison's correspondence with Trist in the 1820s and 1830s on constitutional issues is still used by legal scholars. Trist's behavior in Havana led to his dismissal from that position by Secretary of State Daniel Webster on July 15, 1841 after the publication of two extensive Congressional reports and an on-site investigation. Nevertheless, in 1845, after a period of financial hardship, Trist was appointed Chief Clerk of the State Department, effectively what is now Under Secretary of State, and in that position completed the negotiation of the Treaty of Guadalupe Hildalgo in

Annual importation of slaves into Cuba, which had nearly doubled in the 1810s and 1820s over the previous two decades, increased even further in the 1830s.[19] The slave traders, who conducted business both in Cuba and Spain, laughed off the 1835 Treaty. In his memoirs, Theophilus Conneau, a twenty-year veteran of the slave trade then employed by Pedro Blanco, "the Rothschild of the slave trade," dismissively asserted that "this philanthropic law (if it was such) did not diminish the slave trade one iota, but on the contrary, it drove slavers to use harsher treatment of their slaves…" According to Conneau:

> Spanish slave merchants had recourse to other nations for the protection of their property: Portuguese and Brazilian vessels carried on the Spanish slave trade for a long while, and …Americans took the Spanish cargoes out to Africa for the purchase of the slaves….

1847–1848 against the orders of President James Polk, who, despite its subsequent ratification, was so aggravated that he withheld moneys due to Trist. Many years afterwards Trist obtained passage of a private bill authorizing payment but refused to pay the contingency fee of the lawyer who assisted him in obtaining it, a refusal upheld by the Supreme Court on the ground that the lawyer had been lobbying, not rendering legal services. Wallace Ohrt, *Defiant Peacemaker: Nicholas Trist in the Mexican War* (College Station: Texas A&M University Press, 1997); Robert W. Drexler, *Guilty of Making Peace: A Biography of Nicholas P. Trist* (Lanham, Md.: University Press of America, 1991); "Nicholas P. Trist", Rep. No. 707, H. Rep., 26th Cong., 1st Sess. (1840); "Search and Seizure of American Vessels on the Coast of Africa, &c.", Doc. No. 115, 26th Cong., 2d Sess. , H. Rep., (1841); *Trist v. Child*, 88 U.S. 441 (1874). See Zephyr Teachout, *Corruption in America: From Benjamin Franklin's Snuff Box to Citizens United* (Harvard Univ. Press 2014), 154–158, 271–272.

[19] Drescher, 192, 283. Dale T. Graden, *Disease, Resistance and Lies: The Demise of the Transatlantic Slave Trade to Brazil and Cuba* (Baton Rouge, LSU Press 2014), 149; Alex Borucki, David Eltis and David Wheat, "Atlantic History and the Slave Trade to Spanish America," 120 (2015) *The American Historical Review* 433, 449, 454.

> As slavers could not be fitted out from the Island of Cuba, other nations sent their vessels, ready equipped, to Africa, and there... transferred their vessels to African traders, the Captain and part of the crew taking passage home with their registers in any other lawful trader.[20]

While almost all of the British anti-slavery activity was on the water, there was one spectacular exception: a raid on land at the mouth of the Gallinas River in November 1840 by British Naval forces commanded by Joseph Denman at the request of the Governor to rescue a free black woman named Try Norman and her child—British subjects in Sierra Leone—who had been kidnapped and transported to a barracoon by the eldest son of a local king to be sold as slaves. Denman found and rescued them both and, for good measure, liberated over 800 other captives imprisoned there awaiting sale and burned down the barracoons. Denman later explained in testimony in London before a Parliamentary committee: "I considered that the woman Try Norman was as much a British subject as any person in this room. I can see no distinction between his making a slave of her and his making a slave of any white person."[21]

---

[20] *A Slaver's Log Book, or 20 Years' Residence in Africa: The Original Manuscript by Captain Theophilus Conneau* (Prentice-Hall: Englewood, N.J. 1976), 80–81; Brantz Mayer, *Captain Canot: or, Twenty Years An African Slaver* (London: Routledge 1855), 212; Thomas Fowell Buxton, *The African Slave Trade* (London: Murray, 2d ed. 1839), 21–24, 178–179; Turnbull 379–383.

[21] Testimony of Captain Joseph Denman before the Committee on the West Coast of Africa, June 24, 1842, *Trial of de Zulueta*, 127–128.

Henry John Temple, 3rd Viscount Palmerston

Denman's action beyond her rescue were controversial in some quarters,[22] but not with his father, then Lord Chief Justice of England and an abolitionist, who wrote to two of his other children: "There can be no doubt that the heaviest blow that has ever been aimed at the nefarious traffic has been struck by your brother", although he did acknowledge "possibly … some irregu-

[22] The Queen's Advocate General, responding to a request from the Foreign Secretary, opined: "… Blockading Rivers, landing and destroying Buildings, and carrying off Persons held in Slavery, in Countries with which Great Britain is not at War, cannot be considered as sanctioned by the Law of Nations or by the Provisions of any existing Treaties…" Charles Mitchell and Leslie Turano, "*Buron v. Denman (1848)*" in Charles Mitchell and Paul Mitchell, *Landmark Cases in the Law of Tort* (Oxford: Hart 2010), 33, 55.

larity."[23] However, the effrontery of the slave traders knew no bounds. Four of them brought three actions against Denman personally in the Court of King's Bench in London in 1842 for his destruction of their property in his raid. But when the Great Britain adopted his raid in its entirety as government-sponsored, the first action failed and the others were withdrawn.

Two of these plaintiffs have connections to the purchasers of the *Catharine* in Havana: one was Domingo Martinez, sharing the family name of Pedro Martinez, the principal of Pedro Martinez & Co. of Cadiz and Havana, described in correspondence forwarded by Lord Palmerston to the British ambassador in Madrid as "a notorious slave-merchant at Cadiz... by repute the wealthiest man in that city, ... said to be the owner of no fewer than 30 vessels engaged in that traffic."[24] Pedro Martinez was also co-owner of many other slave ships in association with Pedro Blanco,[25] the "Rothschild of the slave trade". According to Lord Palmerston's cover letter, dated January 7, 1838, these ships carried on the slave trade "at Cadiz and in the West Indies, in vessels which sail under the Portuguese Flag, although they are Spanish property and are reported to belong to a notorious slave-merchant at Cadiz, named Pedro Martinez." Indeed, Palmerston complained to the United States government in February 1838 that an American schooner, sailing to Africa from Havana in November 1837, had been "entered outwards in the names of the great slave dealers, Pedro Martinez and Company."[26] Even Nicholas Trist,

---

[23] Joseph Arnould, *Memoir of Thomas, First Lord Denham, Formerly Lord Chief Justice of England* (London 1873), II, 121.

[24] *British Parliamentary Papers, Accounts and Papers,* 15, Vol. L, Class B, Correspondence with Foreign Powers, Spain, 3–4 (1838). See also Eltis, 148–149.

[25] Mitchell, 43 n. 43.

[26] *Accounts and Papers*, 15, L, Class B, United States, 72.

the suspect American consul in Havana, had written to the Secretary of State, John Forsyth, on January 25, 1839, referring to a vessel as lately "in the service of Pedro Martinez & Co., the most distinguished, perhaps, of all the slave traders of this place."[27]

A second plaintiff in the cases against Captain Denman, Simon Perez de Teran, was described in the April 1840 report from the British Commissioners in Sierra Leone on their condemnation of the brig *Eliza Davidson* as "a leading partner of the house of Pedro Martinez and Company" in Havana. By 1860, Teran was a major sugar planter in Cuba, with 2000 acres and 320 slaves.[28] A third plaintiff, Tomas Rodriguez Buron, whose case was the one tried, had been left behind to look after Pedro Blanco's installation in the Gallinas—established in the 1820s by Blanco with his business partner, Pedro

---

[27] On March 3, 1841, a day before he went out of office, President Van Buren furnished a report to the House of Representatives pursuant to its earlier resolution. The report, Doc. No. 115, 26th Cong. 2d Sess., H. Rep., entitled "Search or Seizure of American Vessels on Coast of Africa, &c.," had been prepared by Forsyth and reproduced correspondence between himself and Trist. However, the letters were identified as "extracts," and the phrase quoted above was deleted. See *id.* at 298. On July 14, 1841, President Tyler forwarded a report to the House of Representatives from his Secretary of State, Daniel Webster, including correspondence omitted from Doc. 115, including "those parts of the dispatches from Nicholas Trist...to the Department of State, not contained in the said message of the 3d of March last," supplying the language quoted above. See Doc. No. 34, 27th Cong., 1st Sess., H. Rep., entitled "Seizure of American Vessels : Slave Trade", 31.

[28] *British Parliamentary Papers, Correspondence with the British Commissioners at Sierra Leone, the Havana, Rio de Janeiro, and Surinam, relating to the Slave Trade, from May 11th, to December 31st., 1840, inclusive* (London: HM Stationery Office 1841), Class A, 73. *Hunt's Merchants' Magazine and Commercial Review*, 43 (1860), 384

Martinez—when Blanco returned to Havana in 1839; it appears that in the litigation he was fronting for Blanco.[29]

Pedro Martinez was no stranger to the British courts. On April 1, 1835, local authorities in Gibraltar arrested as a slave ship the vessel *Cazador*, on a voyage from Cadiz to the African coast and then onwards to Havana, which had stopped there three days earlier to pick up a cargo which included thirty-cases of muskets and six hundred barrels of gunpowder, shipped on orders of Pedro Martinez by his local agent, William Sherwill. After the seizure, an inspection revealed that "the vessel was in every particular fitted and equipped as a vessel for the transport of slaves, and that her fitting and equipment were not compatible with her employment in any other trade whatever."[30]

The Spanish ambassador immediately demanded the release of the *Cazador*, asserting that under the treaty between Spain and Great Britain any proceedings against the vessel had to be held before the Mixed Commission, an assertion Lord Palmerston rejected on the grounds that the charge was "a breach of British Law, committed within British territory…."[31]

Following a trial in the Vice Admiralty Court in Gibraltar on September 26, 1835, on September 29 the judge rejected the denials of Martinez and the others involved, forfeited the *Cazador* and its cargo, and fined Martinez, Sherwill and the two owners of the vessel ten thousand pounds each. Meantime, the day before the forfeiture trial, Sherwill was tried on a criminal indictment for loading cargo on the *Cazador* to be used in

---

[29] Mitchell and Mitchell, 44–45, 49.

[30] *Sherwill v. The King*, 2 *Moore's Privy Council Reports* 1, 2–7 (1836).

[31] *British and Foreign State Papers, 1835–1836,* XXIV (London: Ridgway 1853) 180–183.

the slave trade, convicted, sentenced to three years' imprisonment at hard labor and remanded.

However, when the case reached the Privy Council Sherwill's criminal conviction was reversed because of a failure of proof that he had guilty knowledge of the objective of the vessel. As to Pedro Martinez, the Privy Council concluded that his cargo must be restored to him, since the forfeiture provisions of the statute only applied to the goods belonging to the owner of the vessel, which he was not, and that only one ten thousand pound penalty could be visited jointly on the vessel owner and master.[32]

---

[32] *Del Campo and Martinez v. The Queen*, 2 *Moore's Privy Council Reports*, 14–17 (1837).

CHAPTER 2

August 26, 1839

On August 26, 1839, off the west coast of Africa, after firing a warning cannon shot, the British Navy's H.M.S. *Dolphin* overhauled and boarded the *Butterfly,* a ship recently built in Baltimore, cleared from Havana and flying American colors, which proved to be carrying the planking needed for the easy construction of a "slave deck" and water "leagers", as well as a "boiler" of sufficient size to maintain 300 slaves, far more people than the Spanish crewmen and the American posing as its master, Isaac P. Morris, found on board.[33] Manned by a British prize crew, the *Butterfly* and Morris were dispatched to New York for forfeiture proceedings against the *Butterfly* and criminal proceedings against Morris under American law.

Likewise dispatched to New York for the same purposes, along with its make-believe American master, Frederick A. Peterson, and its Spanish supercargo and real master, Jose Pereya, was the *Catharine,* also newly built in Baltimore and cleared from Havana, identically equipped for the transportation of slaves and hoisting American colors after it failed to outrun the H.M.S. *Dolphin*

---

[33] The owner of the *Butterfly*, Nathan Farnsworth, was already known to the British Navy. On May 31, 1838 he had bought the *Ontario* and on July 17 of the same year the *Traveller.* On June 18, 1839, the *Ontario* was seized with 220 slaves aboard just after transfer to a foreign owner, thus allowing action by the Mixed Commission. *British and Foreign State Papers 1840–1841* (London: Ridgway 1857), XXIX, 255–257.

REGISTER OF VESSELS

In pursuance of an ACT of the CONGRESS of the United States of America entitled AN ACT

Register

Butterfly register
(*Courtesy National Archives, RG 21, New York*)

near Lagos on August 13. The day after the *Catharine* arrived in New York harbor, the Spaniard, Jose Pereya, killed himself by cutting his own throat.

August 26, 1839 is also the day that Lieutenant Thomas Gedney, of the U.S. Navy brig *Washington*, surveying off Montauk, Long Island, sent a boatload of armed sailors to board a suspicious schooner, anchored nearby, named the *Amistad.* Its cargo of African slaves, kidnapped in their native land and carried to Havana for sale,[34] had risen against their captors while on a short second voyage along the Cuban coast for delivery to their purchasers' sugar plantations. They had killed the captain and the cook and demanded that the vessel sail to Africa. The surviving crew members sailed east by day but north by night, hoping for rescue.

Lieut. Gedney's action that day began a course of proceedings culminating in a decision of the Supreme Court of the United States written by Justice Story,[35] several important scholarly books,[36] a website[37] and a

---

[34] The slaves on the *Amistad* had been purchased on the African coast by "Portuguese merchants working for the Cuban house of Martinez, in Havana". David Brion Davis, *Inhuman Bondage–The Rise and Fall of Slavery in the New World* (New York: Oxford University Press 2006), 12–13. According to Benjamin N. Lawrance, *Amistad's Orphans: An Atlantic Story of Children, Slavery and Smuggling* (New Haven: Yale University Press 2014), 41:

> Amistad's orphans found themselves caught in a web of slave trading spun by four Spanish Cubans and their accomplices, with operations and investments in two hemispheres, three continents, and at least five countries and dominions. Like many thousands before them, the children were embroiled in an enterprise spear-headed by Blanco, operated by the Catalan Cuban Jose Ruiz Carrias, financed in part by the Spanish Cuban Pedro Martinez and his investors, and fueled by shipowners Ramon and Damian Ferrer.... Blanco ... had a cemented relationship supplying Martinez and Company with slaves from Galinhas....Ramon Ferrer turned to the Martinez slave vendors in Havana to bring slaves to Puerto Principe. Martinez and Company drew on Blanco for his primary supply....

See also *ibid.*, 119, 123; Michael Zeuske, *Amistad: A Hidden Network of Slavers and Merchants* (Princeton: Marcus Weiner 2015), 73.

[35] 40 U.S. 518 (March 9, 1841).

[36] Howard Jones, *Mutiny on the* Amistad: *The Saga of a Slave Revolt and Its Impact on American Abolition, Law, and Diplomacy* (Oxford 1987); *ibid.*, "The Impact of the *Amistad* Case on Race and Law in America (1841)", in Annette Gordon-Reed, *Race on Trial: Law and Justice in American History* (Oxford 2002), 14; Marcus Rediker, *The*

motion picture released in 1997, directed by Steven Spielberg, with a cameo appearance by Justice Harry Blackmun. In the 175 years since the Supreme Court's decision, the *Amistad* case has never been forgotten. The only other American case involving the international slave trade which approaches the *Amistad's* historical visibility is the *Antelope,* a slave ship boarded by a U. S. Treasury revenue cutter on June 29, 1820, off St. Augustine on the Florida coast, then in Spanish hands, and found to have 280 Africans from Surinam in chains aboard. The aftermath of that seizure similarly included a final adjudication in the Supreme Court[38] and an outstanding scholarly book.[39]

Comparatively little has been written about the proceedings in New York against the *Catharine* and the *Butterfly* and the masters of each, especially in contrast to the *Amistad.* The only substantial discussion of the former two cases, brief as it is, appears in Howard's comprehensive study of the international slave trade in the federal courts in the decades just prior to the Civil War.[40] In one sense that is surprising. For example, while both the *Amistad* and the *Antelope* went to the Supreme Court, so did the prosecution of Isaac Morris on a mid-trial certificate of division.[41] Similarly, while the *Amistad* famously involved John Quincy Adams as counsel at the Supreme Court level, two of Alexander Hamilton's sons,

---

Amistad *Rebellion: An Atlantic Odyssey of Slavery and Freedom* (New York: Viking 2012).

[37] See n. 47.

[38] 23 U.S. 66 (1825).

[39] John T. Noonan, The Antelope: *The Ordeal of the Recaptured Africans in the Administrations of James Monroe and John Quincy Adams* (Berkeley: U.C. Press 1977).

[40] Fehrenbacher, 196 and nn. 122–127, follows Howard. The cases are also briefly mentioned in Martinez, 86–88, 213–214 n. 121, and in her earlier article, "Antislavery Courts and the Dawn of International Human Rights Law", 117 (2008) *Yale L. Rev.* 550, 605 n.240.

[41] 39 U.S. 464 (1840).

Alexander Hamilton, Jr. and his youngest, Philip Hamilton, a name his father had occasion to reuse after his first son by that name died in a duel in 1801, represented both Morris personally and the claimant to the *Butterfly* cargo in the southern district of New York.

Most striking is how interwoven in time and sequence the *Amistad*, the *Catharine* and the *Butterfly* proceedings were in the federal courts, from the beginning to the end. Supreme Court Justice Smith Thompson presided at the initial *habeas corpus* proceedings in the *Amistad* in the circuit court in New Haven on September 20 and 21, 1839, and at the first day of the *Morris* trial in the circuit court for the southern district of New York on November 30, 1839.[42] District Judge Andrew Judson's disposition of the *Amistad* and its slave cargo was in mid-January, 1840.[43] The Supreme Court held oral argument in the *Morris* case on February 17, 1840, and rendered its unanimous opinion eleven days later. Judge Samuel Rossiter Betts's order forfeiting the *Butterfly* occurred on April 7, 1840,[44] and his decision to release the *Catharine*

---

[42] The account of the first day of the *Morris* trial in the December 2, 1839 edition of the *New York Morning Herald* is reprinted in *Accounts and Papers,* 19, XLVII, Class D, Consular (United States), (June 1–December 31, 1839) (1840), 189–192, and reproduced in the Appendix. The report garbles the names of the two cases cited, Sir William Scott's decision in the *Fortuna* in the High Court of Admiralty and Justice Joseph Story's opinion on circuit in *The Alexander*, 1 Fed. Cas. 362 (Case No. 165)(C.C.D. Mass. 1823).

[43] *Gedney v. L'Amistad,* 10 Fed. Cas. 141, 147(Case No. 5,294a) (D. Conn. 1840).

[44] Judge Betts's opinion is not officially reported, but what purports to be his opinion is printed in *British Parliamentary Papers, Correspondence with Foreign Powers,* Class D, 102–106 (May 11 to December 31, 1840), (London: H.M. Stationery Office, 1841), and reproduced in the Appendix. Judge Betts also denied by decree claims asserted for the cargo by Montero, the supercargo, also a client of the Hamiltons. See fn. 76, infra.

Smith Thompson

on August 4, 1840,[45] two days before Morris was convicted in the circuit court of slave trading.[46] Justice Smith Thompson made the final decisions of forfeiture of the *Butterfly* and the *Catharine*, reversing Judge Betts with respect to the latter, on appeal in the circuit court for the southern district of New York just before Christmas, 1840. Arguments in the Supreme Court in the *Amistad*

[45] Judge Betts's opinion, and the opinion of Justice Thompson reversing Judge Betts, are reported together as *United States v. The Catharine,* 25 Fed. Cas. 332 (Case No. 14,755) (S.D.N.Y. 1840, C.C.S.D.N.Y. 1841). Separately disposed of, ultimately favorably, by decree were claims for wages by two members of the crew.

[46] Morris's conviction and his two-year sentence of imprisonment and two thousand dollar fine are reported respectively in *Niles National Register*, 58, 356 (August 8, 1840) and 400 (August 22, 1840).

case began February 20, 1841, and Justice Story's opinion for the Supreme Court was delivered on March 9, 1841; Justice Thompson and Justice Story are the only two justices on the Supreme Court bench for all of the *Antelope, Morris* and *Amistad* cases.

The overlaps between the *Catharine* and the *Amistad* involved more than judges and the timing of proceedings. Richard R. Madden, a dedicated abolitionist until recently one of the British Commissioners in Havana and also appointed Superintendent of Freed Africans liberated by the Mixed Commission there, was in the United States in the fall of 1839. Introduced as an expert witness by the counsel for the *Amistad* slaves, he gave a deposition on November 30, 1839, which was made part of the *Amistad* district court record and clearly influenced the opinion Judge Judson rendered six weeks later. His testimony included the following:

> One of the largest dealers and importers on the island of Cuba, in African slaves, is the notorious house of Martinez & Co. of Havanna and for years past as at present they have been deeply engaged in the traffic; and the Bozal Africans imported by these and all other slave traders when brought to the Havanna are immediately taken to the barracoons or slave marts, five of which are situated in the immediate vicinity of the Governor's country house about one mile and a half from the walls of the Havanna; and from these barracoons they are taken and removed to different parts of the island when sold…[47]

With these many overlaps in time, courts and subject matter, the circumstances of the *Amistad* and the *Catharine*, and their contrasts, help to illuminate the

---

[47] The Amistad Affair: A Trial History– law2.umkc.edu/…/trials/ami stad/AMI (last visited August 27, 2015).

significance and multiple meanings of both. The most dramatic factual distinction between the *Amistad* (and the *Antelope*), on the one hand, and the *Catharine* and the *Butterfly* on the other, explains why the former are unforgettable and the latter almost unknown: at the time of capture there were slaves on both of the *Antelope* and the *Amistad*, but the *Catharine* and the *Butterfly* had yet to load their human cargos when H.M.S. *Dolphin* took them in custody. The absence of slaves on the latter two vessels created central legal issues in the proceedings that later took place in the southern district of New York.

Second, the *Amistad* was captured off Long Island by the United States Navy and sent to New Haven, while the *Butterfly* and the *Catharine* were captured off the west coast of Africa by the British Navy and sailed to New York. Third, the *Amistad* was genuinely a Spanish flag ship on a voyage along the Cuban coast when the slaves aboard rose; the *Butterfly* and the *Catharine,* en route from Havana to Africa, purported to be U.S. flag vessels with American owners, although they had been documented (at the American Consulate), crewed and loaded in Havana.

Finally, despite Great Britain's determined efforts to eradicate the international slave trade, even Lord Palmerston, the Queen's Advocate-General and the Mixed Commission in Sierra Leone, reached demonstrably incorrect legal conclusions affecting the *Catharine* and the *Butterfly*. So did the United States district attorney, Benjamin F. Butler, recently retired as President Andrew Jackson's Attorney General and acting Secretary of War and then also actively engaged in founding what is now New York University Law School. He refused to take legal action against two captured slave ships—the *Eagle* and the *Clara*—dispatched to New York from the African coast by the British Navy just weeks before the *Butterfly*

Benjamin F. Butler
(Courtesy New York Public Library)

and the *Catharine*; his legal analysis in those instances was the same as the one for which Howard taxes Judge Betts. Butler would also have made the judges' job easier by a fuller presentation about the individuals involved with the *Catharine* in Havana.

But that said, prosecute the *Butterfly* and the *Catharine* cases Butler did, and, in the district and circuit courts in the southern district of New York, between them Judge Betts and Justice Thompson condemned both ships and presided at the trial at which Isaac Morris, the captain of the *Butterfly,* was criminally convicted of slave trading. As will be seen, also, neither judge surpassed in rigor Chief Justice Roger Brooke Taney, both in the Supreme Court in the interlocutory appeal in the *Morris* case and presiding in the several trials in United States circuit court in Baltimore brought against the local builders of the *Catharine* by the United States district attorney, Nathaniel Williams. In contrast, in the *Amistad* proceedings in the district court and the Supreme Court, the Van Buren administration represented the interests of the Spanish government in trying to restore the slaves to their Cuban owners, even though Spain openly acknowledged that its obligations under its treaties with Great Britain to end its slave trade were being ignored in Cuba.[48]

So, in contrast to Howard's views, it will be suggested that in the cases arising from the seizures of the *Butterfly* and the *Catharine* the federal judiciary shines compared to other governments and to the other branches of the government of the United States. Particularly outstanding—and not much remembered for it or anything else—is District Judge Andrew Judson, who enforced Spain's treaty with England, denouncing the Spanish government's claim for the slaves on behalf of the Cuban interests which the Van Buren administration had put forward in his court in the *Amistad* case:

> I find, then, as a matter of fact, that in the month of June, 1839, the law of Spain did prohibit, under severe penalty,

---

[48] The Spanish consul was quite honest about it to the district court in New Haven (*ibid.*):

> STATEMENT OF A.G. VEGA, SPANISH CONSUL (January 10, 1840)
>
> That he is a Spanish subject; that he resided in the island of Cuba several years; that he knows the laws of that island on the subject of slavery; that there was no law that was considered in force in the island of Cuba, that prohibited the bringing in African slaves; that the Court of Mixed Commissioners had no jurisdiction except in cases of capture on the sea; that newly imported African negroes were constantly brought to the island, and, after landing, were bona fide transferred from one owner to another, without any interference by the local authorities or the Mixed Commission, and were held by the owners, and recognised as lawful property; that slavery was recognised in Cuba by all the laws that were considered in force there....

> the importation into Cuba of negroes from Africa. These negroes were imported in violation of that law....
>
> This brings me to the question of title in Montez and Ruez, who now claim them through their government.... Why did they not ascertain that these negroes were Bozals. This has been the source of all their complicated sufferings, the tale of which, will make the stoutest heart bleed. Why did they not ascertain that the law of Spain had declared these objects of their purchase not slaves? The secret is told in a word. In Cuba it is the custom to buy such negroes, and ship them as Ladinos or Creoles [indigenous]; and there respectable men have grown up under the influence of this custom—this practice against law. The subjects of a foreign government are presumed, however, to know what their own laws are, and when broken, they cannot come here and ask us to invade the rights of others, in justification of the breach of their own laws. This would not be done, even there. Hence the Spanish consul says this mode of "bona fide" selling is carried on without notice from the local authorities. Not that the act is lawful, in itself, but only because the act is passed over.[49]

Second, the obloquy visited on Judge Betts of the southern district of New York for his decision in the *Catharine* and his disagreement with Justice Story in the early stage of the *Morris* prosecution, viewed in context, is ill-deserved. In each case his hesitation, in participating in the division in the circuit court at the outset of Morris's trial and in dismissing the proceedings against the *Catharine* in the district court, was demonstrably guided by legitimate prudential considerations applied in later cases, even if the results reached in these on appeal were preferable.

---

[49]*Gedney v. L'Amistad, supra,* 10 Fed. Cas. at 146–147.

Last, as already suggested, in the case of the *Catharine*, a more complete presentation of the facts, had they been available, could have led to an immediate condemnation in the district court. The 350 pairs of manacles hidden in two bags in the hold were not discovered there until the vessel was unloaded while the case was on appeal to the circuit court, where the record was reopened to receive this evidence. Similarly, the record in the case does not reflect the fact that the claimant opposing the condemnation of the vessel as its temporary nominal owner, an American resident in Havana named Charles Tyng, was a shipbroker heavily involved in the African slave trade.[50] Nor does it show that Judge Betts was ever told that the first purchaser of the vessel from Tyng, Pedro Martinez and Co., was the most prominent slave trading house in Havana—as Richard Madden had testified in the *Amistad* proceedings in the district court in New Haven eight months before—or that Simon Perez de Teran, the individual identified by name as the final purchaser, after Pedro Martinez and Co. purported to rescind its purchase, was himself "a leading partner" in Pedro Martinez and Co.; or that the purported charterer of the *Catharine* for its outward voyage to Africa flying the American flag, John S. Thrasher, was a clerk in Tyng's own office barely of legal age.

---

[50] By the early spring 1840, before Judge Betts decided the case in August, Tyng had been identified as involved, with Simon Perez de Teran, in shipping the cargo on three other slave ships intercepted by the British Navy off the coast of Africa before loading slaves, the *Asp,* the *Lark* and the *Eliza Davidson*; Teran was a part owner of the *Lark.* In July 1840, Tyng also had signed consular documents in Havana to clear five other slave ships: the *Hudson, Plant, Lone, Seminole* and *Kite. Correspondence with the British Commissioners,* Class A, 28–30, 73–76, 153–160; Doc. No. 115, 226–228; Graden, 30, 115.

CHAPTER 3

The First New York Cases

In 1839 the British Commissioners in Sierra Leone had no wish to be involved in a contretemps with the American government over British Naval detention of an increasing number of slave ships flying the American flag, and so they refused to assert jurisdiction over such vessels brought to the Mixed Commission by the British Navy. H.W. Macaulay, who had been the British Commissary judge in Sierra Leone from the end of 1831 to the end of 1839, testified as follows before the Parliamentary Commission in June 1842:

> Have there been a considerable number of restorations; can you state, from statistics, the number? —I have statistics for two years; from the 1st of January to the 31st of December 1838, one vessel only was liberated.
>
> What number were condemned? —Forty-one; during the year 1839, there were two liberated, and 45 condemned; and in addition to those, there was a very large number of American vessels which were seized, with American papers on board, and which I refused to receive into court at all; there were some in 1838, and there was a large number in 1839.
>
> Can you state the number? —I think the number was 13; but the reports of the whole of those cases are in the Parliamentary Papers.

> Were they *bona fide* American? —I believe not American, in any one case, but sailing under the American flag, with American papers, supplied to them by American authority.
>
> Where? —Almost entirely, I think, without one exception, at Havannah.
>
> Supplied by the American consul? Yes; but I considered that as they sailed with those American papers, however wrongfully they might have been given by the American authority, we had no right to interfere with them.
>
> ***
>
> But in those cases which you mention, you had not the slightest doubt in the world that they would have been condemned if they had not had American papers on board? —Certainly they would...but none of the cases I speak of were prosecuted; I would not allow them to be libeled in court.[51]

Macaulay had made his views clear at the time. For example, writing to Lord Palmerston under date of April 15, 1839, he said:

> We have the honour to report to your Lordship, that another vessel has been detained whilst sailing under the American flag, and has been sent in for adjudication. ...
>
> The detained schooner arrived at Sierra Leone on the 23rd ultimo, and an attempt was made two days later to bring her case before the British and Spanish Mixed Court of Justice; but, as the captor's declaration stated especially that the vessel was "sailing under American

---

[51] *Trial of De Zueleta*, 10–11, Nos. 5016–5021, 5024.

Slave Ship
(*Poems on the Abolition of the Slave Trade*, London: Bowyer 1809)

colours" at the time of her detention, we felt bound to follow the same course which had been adopted in the cases of the "*Mary Anne Cassard*," "*Florida*," "*Hazard*," and "*Eagle*," and we did not admit the captor's allegations to proof, considering that it was not competent for the Court to proceed upon information, obtained by the unauthorized visitation and search of a vessel belonging to a power, which had not conceded to our cruizers the right which in this instance was exercised.

> In the four cases referred to, there was abundant reason to believe that the captor's allegations, as to the fraudulent assumption of the American flag, would have been proved, even from the papers produced, if the opportunity for doing so had been afforded....[52]

The *Eagle*

A slave ship built for the purpose in Baltimore in 1837, with a wholly Spanish crew and flying American colors, the *Eagle*—referred to in the letter above—had been detained on the African coast on January 14, 1839 by the HMS *Lily*, commanded by John Reeve, and sent on to Sierra Leone with Joshua W. Littig, the sole American on board who was posing as her captain, under the command of a prize master, G.S. Boys, and a prize crew. Boys described the vessel as "*perfectly* completed for the reception of a cargo of many hundred human beings; *her-slave-deck-laid,* provisions on board, besides coppers, irons, &c." Once in Sierra Leone, Boys consulted Dougan, the British agent there, who:

> was of opinion that the vessel having shown American colours... there would be an objection against her being taken into court, but that there could be no doubt at the same time as to her being a Spanish vessel, and that the American flag was only hoisted as a decoy to the men-of-war, the Mixed Commission having no authority to act over any vessel showing American Colours. On the fourth day after my arrival there, a petition was sent into Court by Mr. Dougan, praying that the "Eagle" might be tried, which petition was thrown out.[53]

---

[52] *Correspondence with the British Commissioners,* Class A, 32.
[53] *Accounts and Papers*, 19, XLVII, Class D, 127.

The British Commissioners' report to Lord Palmerston about the *Eagle*, noting that the *Lily* was the fourth British warship to "attempt to bring this vessel into the British and Spanish Mixed Court of Justice" in the previous three months, advised that this effort "was frustrated by Her Majesty's Commissioners, who considered that Captain Reeve's acknowledgment, that the *Eagle* was captured under the flag and pass of The United States, decisive as to the non-admissibility of the case, into any of the Courts over which they are appointed to preside."[54]

Boys set off with Littig in the *Eagle* in a vain search for the *Lily* but seems instead to have found HMS *Buzzard,* commanded by Lieutenant Charles Fitzgerald. By this time Littig was already losing his nerve, Boys reporting that Littig had said several times in his presence: "'Well [B]oys, they can only put me in prison, and I shall lose all my wages,' the tears at this time falling down from his eyes." To Fitzgerald Littig made a statement, reduced to writing by Fitzgerald and signed by Littig, that the *Eagle* was Spanish and, when captured, loading provisions for a cargo of slaves, his presence as captain and the American flag intended to provide protection against detention by the British Navy. Littig also asserted that he had been retained for the purpose in Havana, and that the bill of sale naming him as owner found on board "he supposes was transacted in the United States Consul's Office in Havana, without his being privy to it." The vessel and its clearance was fully documented at the United States Consulate in Havana, with a certificate from Consul Nicholas Trist giving a false destination.[55]

---

[54] *British and Foreign State Papers* 1839–1840, XXVIII (1857), 479.
[55] *Accounts and Papers,* XLVII, Class D, 128–129; *British and Foreign State Papers,* XXVIII, 479–480.

The *Clara*

On March 18, 1839, less than a week after taking charge of the *Eagle*, Lieutenant Fitzgerald boarded and the next day detained the *Clara*, which had been built in Baltimore for Francis T. Montell and transferred to its ostensible American captain, Samuel B. Hooker, by a bill of sale authenticated by the American vice-consul at Havana on October 28, 1838. When detained, the *Clara* was at anchor just off the coast, fitted out for the carriage of slaves, with eighty slaves already acquired ashore by the supercargo (a Spaniard and the real captain) and waiting in a barracoon to be loaded aboard from canoes. Hooker acknowledged that he had been engaged by a Havana slave trader to provide cover for the vessel as American.

Although intending to bring the *Eagle* and the *Clara* to the Mixed Commission in Freetown, in April 1839 Fitzgerald was ordered to sail them both to New York, along with the Americans posing as their captains, for delivery to the United States government.[56] Fitzgerald reached there in June, and not long after their arrival, Hooker killed himself.

The *Wyoming*

On June 29, the *Wyoming*, separately seized in similar circumstances in mid-May in the Gallinas River on the west coast of Africa, arrived in New York for the same purpose, her American "captain" having died the day after

---

[56] *Accounts and Papers,* 17, XLII, Class A, 51–52; Doc. 115, 92–98. The British commander believed that it was imperative to demonstrate how the American flag was being abused by slave traders.

her capture "from the bursting of a blood-vessel." The British naval officer in charge reported to the British Consul in New York on arrival that when captured the *Wyoming* had on board her American "captain", a Spanish crew of ten, fourteen alleged Spanish passengers, "enormous casks for water (capable of containing three tuns each), a slave-deck, marked and numbered, and a very large quantity of rice."[57]

Following the arrival in New York of these three ships, the British Ambassador wrote to the Acting Secretary of State, providing documentary evidence from the Royal Navy and inviting the intervention of the judicial authorities of the United States. The latter promptly replied that the President—"impelled by the same feeling of abhorrence of the inhuman traffic" and "anxious that no means within his reach shall be left untried to prevent or punish infractions of the law of the United States for the suppression of the slave trade"—had directed that the information so provided be delivered to "the public prosecutor", in this case Benjamin F. Butler, the United States district attorney for the southern district of New York.[58]

The British Consul in New York, James Buchanan, met with Butler and reported to Lord Palmerston on June 29 that:

> The course to be pursued has not yet been decided on, as the laws are very defective, and only by construction reach the case of any of these vessels; for though fitted out as Slavers, and avowedly on the coast for the purpose, yet no Slaves being found on board, nor the ship fitted out in the United States for Slaves, there is a

---

[57] Doc. 115, 100–101.
[58] *Accounts and Papers,* XLVII, Class D, 138.

> difficulty in the technicality of the statute of reaching these particular cases.[59]

On July 30, the British Ambassador wrote to Lord Palmerston that he understood Butler to be "of opinion that all these vessels may be proceeded against as American Slavers, with a reasonable prospect of their conviction under the law of the United States, which pronounces Slave-trading to be Piracy...."[60] But by letter dated August 9, 1839, Butler declined to proceed against the *Eagle* and the *Clara:*

> The following matters appear on these papers;
>
> 1. That the vessels were built and registered at Baltimore. The register of the "Eagle" is dated December 1, 1837, and that of the "Clara" July 27, 1838.
>
> 2. That the vessels being afterwards in the port of Havana, they were transferred, at the office of the American consul of that port—the "Eagle" to Joshua W. Littig, and the "Clara" to Samuel B. Hooker; the bill of sale, in each case, being executed by the master of the vessel named in the register, acting by virtue of a power of attorney from the owners.
>
> 3. Littig and Hooker are represented by the papers to be American citizens. They respectively assumed the command of the vessels transferred to them, as masters thereof; and they were in command when the vessels were examined and detained by the British cruisers.
>
> 4. Although on the face of the papers, the vessels are thus reported as American property, there is the best

---

[59] *Ibid.,* 139
[60] *Ibid.,* 148–149.

> reason to believe that they were actually owned by Spanish subjects, and that the names of the American citizens were used as a mere cover to conceal the true ownership; and such, after a careful and deliberate examination of the subject, is my own decided belief.
>
> This conclusion is founded not only on the full acknowledgments made by Littig and Hooker to Lieut. Commandant Fitzgerald, and the other facts set for the in the documents laid before the State Department...but on an inspection of various memoranda and other documents in the Spanish language, laid before me with the ship's papers....
>
> Under these circumstances, I do not think myself authorized by your instructions to proceed against the vessels...

However, Butler did proceed against Joshua W. Littig individually. According to his August 9 letter, Butler obtained an indictment against Littig:

> founded on the 2d and 3d sections of the act of the 10th of May, 1800. In the view I first took of the case, I did not believe this act applied, because no slaves were ever *actually* transported in, or brought on board of, or procured for, Littig's vessel; and I am strongly inclined to this opinion. But as it has been held by Mr. Justice Story, in an information against a vessel under the 1st section of this act, that it is not necessary, to constitute an offense against that section, that slaves should have been taken on board, I have so far changed this opinion as to procure the indictment.[61]

---

[61] 2 Stat. 70. "An Act in addition to an Act entitled "An Act to prohibit the carrying on the Slave-trade from the United States to any foreign Place or Country":

> SEC. 1. Be it enacted...That it shall be unlawful for any citizen of the United States, or other person residing within the United States, directly or indirectly to hold or have any right or property

Butler also advised that he had previously brought a civil action against Littig under the act of 1794, but had concluded he could not establish that the *Eagle* had been built in Baltimore "with the *express design* of being employed as a slaver." However, as Littig was not in custody, Butler obtained a warrant for his arrest on the indictment.[62]

> in any vessel employed or made use of in the transportation or carrying of slaves from one foreign country or place to another, and any right or property, belonging as aforesaid, shall be forfeited, and may be libelled and condemned for the use of the person who shall sue for the same; and such person, transgressing the prohibition aforesaid, shall also forfeit and pay a sum of money equal to double the value of the right or property in such vessel, which he held as aforesaid; and shall also forfeit a sum of money equal to double the value of the interest which he may have had in the slaves, which at any time may have been transported or carried in such vessel, after the passing of this act, and against the form thereof.
>
> SEC. 2. *And be it further enacted,* That it shall be unlawful for any citizen of the United States or other person residing therein, to serve on board any vessel of the United States employed or made use of in the transportation or carrying of slaves from one foreign country or place to another: and any such citizen or other person, voluntarily serving as aforesaid, shall be liable to be indicted therefor, and on conviction thereof shall be liable to a fine not exceeding two thousand dollars, and be imprisoned not exceeding two years.
>
> SEC. 3. *And be it further enacted,* That if any citizen of the United States shall voluntarily serve on board any foreign ship or vessel, which shall hereafter be employed in the slave trade, he shall, on conviction thereof, be liable to and suffer the like forfeitures, pains, disabilities and penalties as he would have incurred, had such ship or vessel been owned or employed, in whole or in part, by any person or persons residing within the United States.

[62] Doc. 115, 102–103. What happened to the Littig prosecution appears to be lost. Lieutenant Fitzgerald wrote to the British Ambassador on September 21, 1839, that Littig "having represented to Mr. Butler...that his mother lately died at Baltimore, where he now is, and requested through his counsel, that his trial may be postponed for a few weeks, Mr. Butler has consented thereto, but on

Under date of August 15, although on somewhat different underlying facts, Butler sent a letter declining to take action against the *Wyoming* for the same reason. However, as Lord Palmerston later informed the British Ambassador, "an informality having been discovered in her papers, she was, on the ground of that informality," condemned in the district court for the southern district of New York based on the libel filed by Butler on September 2, 1839, and Judge Betts's decree, dated October 15, 1839.[63]

The rest of the story of the *Eagle* and the *Clara* is a painful one. Lieutenant Fitzgerald was ordered to take them to the Vice Admiralty Court in Bermuda; the *Eagle* was blown ashore in a gale, and the Vice Admiralty Court refused to accept jurisdiction of the *Clara*. In November Fitzgerald set out from Bermuda in the *Buzzard* with the *Clara* and the *Eagle* again, this time back to the Mixed Commission in Sierra Leone. The vessels were caught in a gale at sea; the *Eagle* sank and the *Clara* was separated from the *Buzzard*. But Fitzgerald soldiered on in the *Buzzard* and filed claims. The Mixed

---

the condition that the evidences of myself and officers are taken *now....*" *Accounts and Papers,* XLVII, Class D, 159. The National Archives case file contains those evidences, similarly dated (although not the indictment) but nothing else. There is no further report in any source of any further proceedings. It may just be coincidence but a Google search under Joshua Wells Littig turns up a tombstone of a man by that name, a native of Baltimore, born there in 1815, and dying in Corpus Christi, Texas in 1870, said to have been one of its earliest settlers – *in the winter of 1839–1840.* (www.cclibrary.com/local history; visited September 6, 2015) In 1839–1840 and for six years thereafter Texas was an independent republic not part of the United States.

[63] *Accounts and Papers,* 19, XLVII, Class D, 157–158; *Correspondence with Foreign Powers,* Class D, 71–74.The grounds for the forfeiture were the failure to comply with the reporting requirements of "An Act concerning the registry and recording of Ships and Vessels" (December 31, 1792), 1 Stat. 287, in connection with the transfer of the *Wyoming* in Havana prior to leaving for the African coast.

Commission condemned the *Eagle* immediately, but waited in vain for eleven months to see if the *Clara* turned up. With a change of British Mixed Commission personnel and Lord Palmerton's pointed advice by letter of September 5, 1839, that Her Majesty's Advocate-General had disapproved the rule announced in the *Mary Anne Cassard* and its progeny refusing to take jurisdiction of slave ships captured while flying American colors, the Mixed Commission this time had no trouble in condemning *in absentia* the *Eagle* and the *Clara* in January and December 1840, respectively.[64]

[64] *British Foreign and State Papers,* XXVIII, 487; *Accounts and Papers*, 17, XLII, 51–60.

CHAPTER 4

The Catharine *and the* Butterfly

Initial Proceedings in New York

The detention of the *Catharine* and the *Butterfly*, both by Lieutenant Holland of HMS *Dolphin,* were virtually contemporaneous with Benjamin Butler's refusals to proceed against the *Eagle* and the *Clara*, but Holland had no way to know that. What he did know was that the Court of Mixed Commission would not take jurisdiction of either capture, and so after briefly calling at Freetown at the end of August, he sent the two ships to New York. The *Catharine* arrived in New York City in mid-October after a 39-day journey at sea, with four of her original crew on board.[65] Her ostensible captain, Frederick Adolph Peterson:

> was brought up and examined at the United States Marshal's office, on a warrant issued on the complaint of Robert H. Dundas, of her Britannic majesty's brig Dolphin. The Catharine had been fitted out at Havannah, cleared there, and the necessary papers obtained through the office of the American vice-consul. The cargo consisted of tobacco and spirits; her crew of six American seamen and of twenty-five Spaniards. The latter were shipped, doubtless, for actual service on the coast of Africa. The Catharine is said to be owned by Messrs. Thomas Wilson and Co., of Baltimore, a

---

[65] *Niles' National Register*, 57, 119 (October 13, 1839).

> branch of a London house. The clearance and necessary papers were obtained at the Havannah, by a person named Ting [sic], who acted as their agent there. The Dolphin fell in with her on the 13th of August, off the coast of Africa.... She gave her chase, and compelled her to bring to by firing several shots. The Dolphin boarded her, and found, that though she was sailing under American colours, she had the necessary planks for a slave-deck, and all other equipments usually found on board a vessel engaged in the slave-trade. No slaves were found on board...
>
> The accused was committed, in default of bail in the sum of 3,000 dollars. The supercargo of the schooner killed himself by cutting his throat.[66]

The arrival of the *Butterfly* and her pretended American captain, Isaac Morris, must have occurred at about

---

[66] *The Annual Register, or a View of the History and Politics of the year 1839*, (October, 1839), 200 (London: Rivington, 1840). A separate account attributed to an unidentified "American newspaper" and republished in *The Sessional Papers, Accounts and Papers,* XIX (1840), 161–162, reports this proceeding as in the "United States Circuit Court, before Justice Kirtland." Ambrose Kirtland was an assistant justice of the City of New York who held the court for the First District on Fulton Street. Apart from reproducing the text of a "secret letter of instructions" found on Peterson's person said to be in the handwriting of "Charles Syng [sic], who in other papers subscribed himself as agent of owners of the vessel," this article reports that all of the Spaniards aboard made their escape when the vessel was detained; that 400 pewter spoons, $2,500 in specie and the makings of a slave deck were found aboard; that the suicide of the supercargo, Jose "Pereja", had occurred the previous Saturday; and that there was a preliminary skirmish between Butler and Francis B. Cutting, counsel for Peterson, about the applicability of the Act of 1800.

the same time, but no report has been located. According to *Niles National Register*:[67]

> The captain of the schooner Butterfly, which was captured as a slaver...on the coast of Africa by the brig, Dolphin, was examined lately by judge Betts, of the United States court. It appeared from the evidence that the vessel was cleared at New Orleans on the 24th of May, 1839, with Nathan Farnsworth as captain, and several American seamen.—The transfer at Havana, was certified by John A. Smith, United States vice consul. On the 28th of June she came into the possession of Morris, who with two mates and six Spanish seamen, sailed for the coast of Africa on the 1st of July, by way of St. Thomas. A Spaniard named Montero officiated as supercargo. When the schooner was taken off Cape St. Paul's, there were found two log books, the one written in English and the other in the Spanish language. The cargo consisted of powder, rum and tobacco. The vessel was arranged after the manner in which slavers are usually built; with slave decks, water casks and boilers, sufficient to accommodate more than two hundred persons.—There were, however, no slaves on board[.] The coun[se]l for the defence submitted to the court whether, there never having been any slaves on the Butterfly, the intent to become a slaver would justify confiscation of the vessel. Judge Betts said the point was worthy of consideration, and he would take time to decide upon the case.
>
> A decision was subsequently made by his honor judge Betts in this case. On consideration of the matter he thought there were not circumstances to warrant his deciding positively whether capt. Morris had made himself amenable to the laws against traffic[k]ing in slaves or not, but that there was sufficient evidence against him

---

[67] November 30, 1839, 223. The same page contains a report that the deposition of Richard Madden had been taken in New Haven in the *Amistad* case on consent.

to warrant his sending this case before the grand jury, and he should then direct that capt. Morris be held to bail in the sum of $4,000 to appear when called upon.

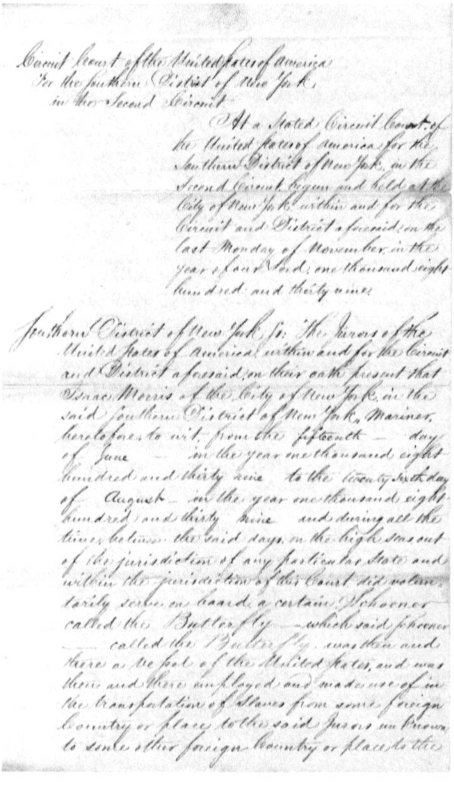
Circuit Court of the United States of America
For the Southern District of New York,
in the Second Circuit
At a Stated Circuit Court of
the United States of America for the
Southern District of New York, in the
Second Circuit begun and held at the
City of New York within and for the
Circuit and District aforesaid, on the
last Monday of November in the
year of our Lord, one thousand eight
hundred and thirty nine:
Southern District of New York ss: The Jurors of the
United States of America, within and for the Circuit
and District aforesaid, on their oath present that
Isaac Morris of the City of New York in the
said Southern District of New York, Mariner,
heretofore, to wit, from the fifteenth — day
of June — in the year one thousand eight
hundred and thirty nine to the twenty sixth day
of August — in the year one thousand eight
hundred and thirty nine and during all the
time between the said days, on the high seas out
of the jurisdiction of any particular State and
within the jurisdiction of this Court, did volun-
tarily serve on board a certain Schooner
called the Butterfly — which said Schooner
— called the Butterfly was then and
there a vessel of the United States, and was
there and there employed and made use of in
the transportation of Slaves from some foreign
Country or place to the said Jurors unknown
to some other foreign Country or place to the

Indictment of Isaac Morris, page 1
(*Courtesy National Archives, RG 21, New York*)

James Buchanan, the British Consul in New York, had informed Lord Palmerston by letter of November 15, 1839, that "Mr. Butler has received instructions from his Government to prosecute the masters, being citizens, [and] also to condemn the vessels for having fraudulently obtained certain papers found on board."[68]

---

[68] *Accounts and Papers*, 19, XLVII, Class D, 184.

The Trial of Isaac Morris

Part One

The grand jury for the United States circuit court acted promptly. Parallel indictments were filed on November 29, 1839, against both Peterson and Morris, following the model that Butler had described in his letter of August 9 regarding Littig: one count of serving on a vessel of the United States employed in the slave trade, being an American citizen, the second count the same except that their vessel was alleged to be a "foreign ship or vessel," in violation of the Act of May 10, 1800.

Morris's trial commenced in the circuit court before Justice Thompson and Judge Betts on November 30, 1839, the day after the indictment came down. The speed with which it came on, and its outcome, suggests an earlier consensus among the judges and the counsel that the issue was one of law, rather than fact. The Court summarily rebuffed efforts by the defense to force the Government to elect between counts and to dismiss the indictment on the grounds that the *Butterfly* had been illegally seized by the British Navy. Butler presented testimony from British naval personnel about the apprehension of the *Butterfly,* the lumber she carried for fabrication of a slave deck and eighteen leagers capable of holding 250 to 300 gallons of water each, and various documents found on board. One of Morris's counsel, Francis B. Cutting, emphasized in brief cross examinations that there were no slaves on board the *Butterfly* and called one witness—on the citizenship of Nathan Farnsworth, the owner who transferred command of the vessel in Havana on June 17, 1839, prior to the vessel's departure for the African coast. There followed a debate between Butler and Morris's other counsel, Alexander Hamilton, Jr., about whether it was an element of the offense that slaves were

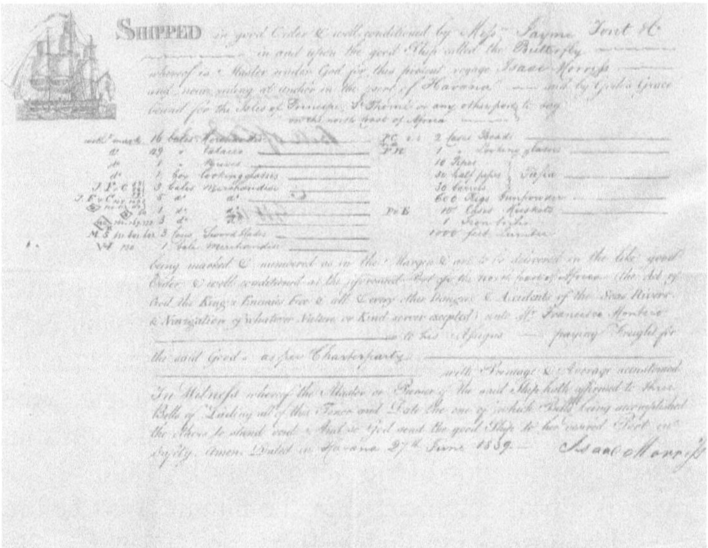
SHIPPED in good Order & well conditioned by
in and upon the good Ship called the Butterfly
whereof is Master under God for this present voyage Isaac Morris
and now riding at anchor in the port of Havana — and by God's Grace
bound for the Isles of Principe, St Thomé or any other port
on the north coast of Africa

being marked & numbered as in the Margin & are to be delivered in the like good
Order & well conditioned at the aforesaid Port
and the King's Enemies Fire & all & every other Dangers & Accidents of the Seas Rivers
& Navigation of whatever Nature or Kind soever excepted
to his Assigns — paying Freight for
the said Goods as per Charterparty
with Primage & Average accustomed
In Witness whereof the Master or Purser of the said Ship hath affirmed to three
Bills of Lading all of this Tenor and Date the one of which Bills being accomplished
the others to stand void. And so God send the good Ship to her desired Port in
safety. Amen. Dated in Havana 27th June 1839 — Isaac Morris

Butterfly bill of lading
(*Courtesy National Archives, RG 21, New York*)

actually on board the vessel and the correctness of Justice Story's decision on circuit sixteen years earlier that it was not. Following this argument:

> The Court said that though they might differ in their views from Judge Story, yet comity required that, as they were circuit judges, of equal jurisdiction, their opinions should not clash; and it was therefore important that the true construction of these laws should be understood throughout the several States; and, in this view, and the Court had concluded to decide in the present case, and to send their opinion to the Supreme Court of the United States for its ultimate adjudication.
>
> It was then agreed by the Counsel on both sides that it was difficult to procure the attendance of the foreign witnesses; that their testimony, in case the decision of Judge Story should be sustained by the Supreme Court, should be used on the future trial of the present case, and that the jury should be discharged

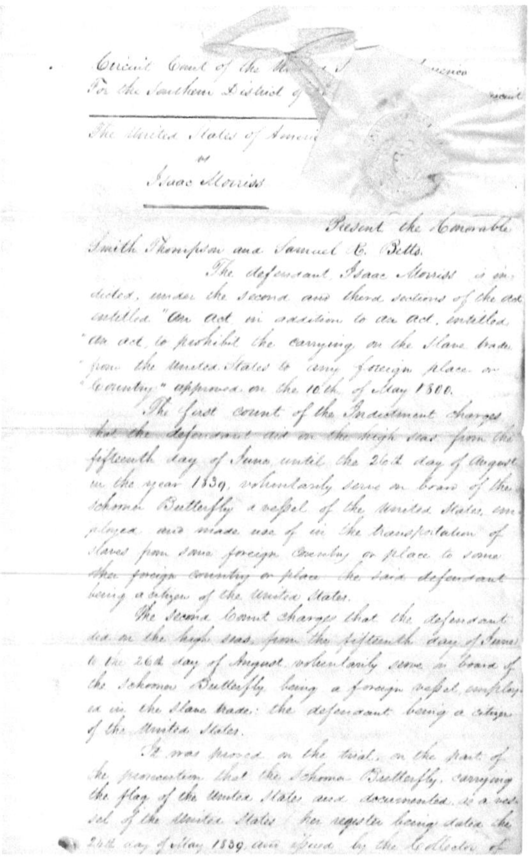
Circuit Court of the [illegible] America
For the Southern District of [illegible]

The United States of America
vs
Isaac Morris

Present the Honorable
Smith Thompson and Samuel R. Betts.

The defendant Isaac Morris is indicted, under the second and third sections of the act entitled "An Act in addition to an act, entitled "An act to prohibit the carrying on the Slave trade "from the United States to any foreign place or "Country" approved on the 10th of May 1800.

The first count of the Indictment charges that the defendant did on the high seas from the fifteenth day of June until the 26th day of August in the year 1839, voluntarily serve on board of the Schooner Butterfly a vessel of the United States, employed and made use of in the transportation of slaves from some foreign Country or place to some other foreign country or place the said defendant being a citizen of the United States.

The second Count charges that the defendant did on the high seas, from the fifteenth day of June to the 26th day of August voluntarily serve on board of the Schooner Butterfly being a foreign vessel, employed in the slave trade: the defendant being a citizen of the United States.

It was proved on the trial, on the part of the prosecution that the Schooner Butterfly, carrying the flag of the United States and documented as a vessel of the United States (her register being dated the 24th day of May 1839 and issued by the Collector of

Certificate of division in *Morris*, page 1
(*Courtesy National Archives, RG 21, New York*)

without a verdict, and the prisoner remanded; also that the case of Peterson take the same course.[69]

---

[69] *Accounts and Papers*, 19, XLVII, 189–192. Until after the Civil War there was no appeal to the Supreme Court from the judgment of a circuit court in a criminal case. All the judges could do, and what they did here, was to certify that they "were opposed in opinion on certain points or questions," which the Supreme Court would then decide. Doing so in the midst of a case, as here, had been discouraged by the Supreme Court in *United States v. Gooding,* 25 U.S. 460 (1827), a slave trade prosecution in the circuit court for the district of Maryland under the 1818 statute.

On December 20, both Morris and Peterson were released on $550.00 bail.[70]

The documentation which accompanied the *Morris* case to the Supreme Court—and which is reproduced at the beginning of the report of its decision—included a statement of the proof at trial, reciting that the register for the *Butterfly* was issued to Nathan Farnsworth, a citizen of the United States, as owner; that, when the vessel was detained, Morris had represented himself as in command and an American citizen; and that:

> No slaves were found on board the vessel at the time of her capture, and it was testified by the witnesses for the prosecution that from the cargo and situation in which the vessel was found no slaves could have been carried or transported in her at any time during the voyage on which she was then engaged: that it would have been necessary to have discharged the cargo before slaves could have been taken on board...

Nevertheless, exactly one month later, on December 30, 1839, Butler commenced forfeiture proceedings in the district court against each of the *Catharine* and the *Butterfly* under the relevant Acts of Congress of 1794, 1800 and 1818 prohibiting participation in the slave trade. The very next day, December 31, 1839, Lord Palmerston struck his colors, writing to the British Consul in New York to report the Queen's Advocate-General's opinion with respect to the *Catharine* and the *Butterfly*: "...neither the vessels nor their cargoes were by the Law of the United States liable to condemnation for being engaged in the Slave Trade...." Palmerston concluded:

> It appears therefore useless for British cruisers to send to the United States any vessels which may be found

---

[70] Circuit court docket book, Dec. 20, 1839.

> equipped for the Slave Trade, even if they had the right, of which they are clearly not possessed, of capturing American vessels so engaged; and the instructions which under the circumstances I have to give you is, that for the future you are not to take charge of such vessels.

The Catharine *in Baltimore*

Both the *Catharine* and the *Butterfly* had been recently built in Baltimore and then taken promptly to Havana and sold into the slave trade, so those involved in their construction must have felt concern at their recent return to the United States in the custody of the British Navy. An October news report which they must have sponsored appeared in the Baltimore *American* and was picked up by *Niles National Register* on November 2, 1839:[71]

> *Case of the Schooner Catharine.* The attention of the public has, of late, been so frequently called to this vessel, and the circumstances under which she has been captured and sent to New York, that we are happy to have it in our power to publish a correct statement of the matter. The facts are simply these.
>
> The schooner *Catharine*, Wm. S. Wedge, master, was dispatched from Baltimore early in May last for Havana, the captain having instructions to value upon one of the most respectable houses there, and to sell the vessel, provided a suitable price was offered for her; —otherwise, to

---

[71] Vol. 57, 159.

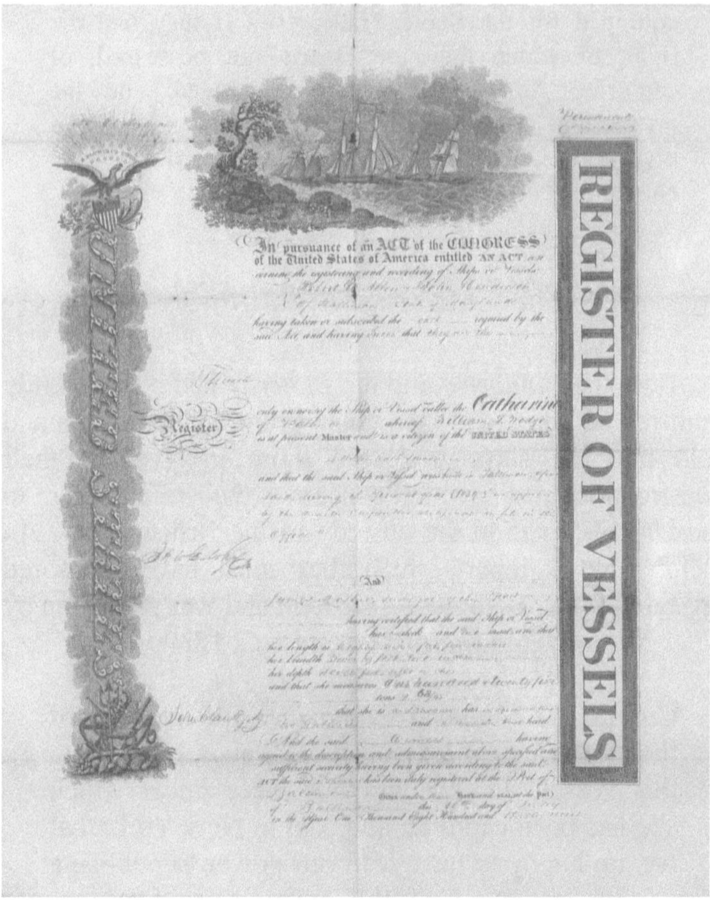

Catharine register
(*Courtesy National Archives, RG 21, New York*)

accept of any good *freight for the United States*, giving preference for direct employment to Baltimore. The consignees being unsuccessful in their endeavors to procure a purchaser at the captain's limits, recommended him to a ship broker, as a person better suited to enable him to accomplish a sale. With the aid of a broker, a *bona fide* sale was made of the vessel, the contract ratified, the money paid, and remittances regularly forwarded

Catharine register verso
(*Courtesy National Archives, RG 21, New York*)

and received by the agents and owners in Baltimore. Captain Wedge, having deposited his register with the United States consul, and received from the consul a receipt for the regular discharge of his seamen, and the payment of three months extra wages according to law, returned directly to the United States.

Here ended all connection of the original owners of the Catharine with this vessel or her subsequent voyage; and such being the fact, they could have no agent to act for them in any business in which they were not in the most indirect manner concerned.

The consular and other documents submitted to our inspection, prove the correctness of what is here alleged, and we are satisfied that the transaction, so far as the parties here are concerned, has been of a correct and mercantile character, and that no suspicion or censure should in any way rest upon them.

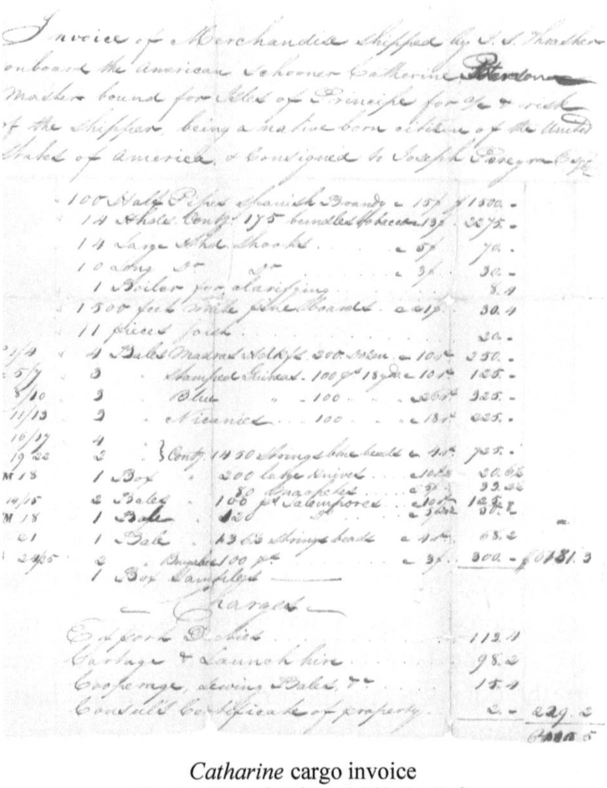
Invoice of Merchandise Shipped by S. S. Thrasher onboard the American Schooner Catherine [illegible] Master bound for Isles of Principe for a/c & risk of the Shipper, being a native born citizen of the United States of America, & Consigned to Joseph [illegible] Esq.

	100 Half Pipes Spanish Brandy	@ 15$	$1500. –
	14 Whole Cont.g 175 bundles tobacco	19$	2275. –
	14 Large Whol. Shooks	@ 5$	70. –
	10 Long D.o D.o	@ 3$	30. –
	1 Boiler for clarifying		8.4
	1500 feet white pine Boards	@ 2$	30.4
	11 pieces [illegible]		20. –
1/4	4 Bales Madras Hdkfs. 200 Dozen	@ 10$	250. –
5/7	3 Stamped Guineas. 100 p.s 18 yds	@ 10$	125. –
8/10	3 Blue 100	@ 26$	325. –
11/13	3 Nicanees 100	@ 18$	225. –
16/17, 19 22	4, 2 } Cont.g 1450 Strings blue beads	@ 4$	725. –
M 18	1 Box 200 large knives	@ [illegible]	20.66
	80 [illegible]	@ 5$	33.33
14/15	2 Bales 100 p.s Salempores	@ 10$	125. –
M 18	1 Bale 120	@ [illegible]	30. –
21	1 Bale 1363 Strings beads	@ 4$	68.2
24/25	2 Bungales 100 p.s	@ 3$	300. – $6181.3
	1 Box Samples		

— Charges —

Export Duties	112.1
Cartage & Launch hire	98.2
Cooperage, sewing Bales, &c	15.1
Consul's Certificate of property	2. – 229.2
	6[illegible] 5

Catharine cargo invoice
(*Courtesy National Archives, RG 21, New York*)

The public relations campaign failed. On November 15, the Grand Jury of the circuit court for the district of

Maryland returned a presentment for Robert W. Allen, on which an arrest warrant issued and which, on November

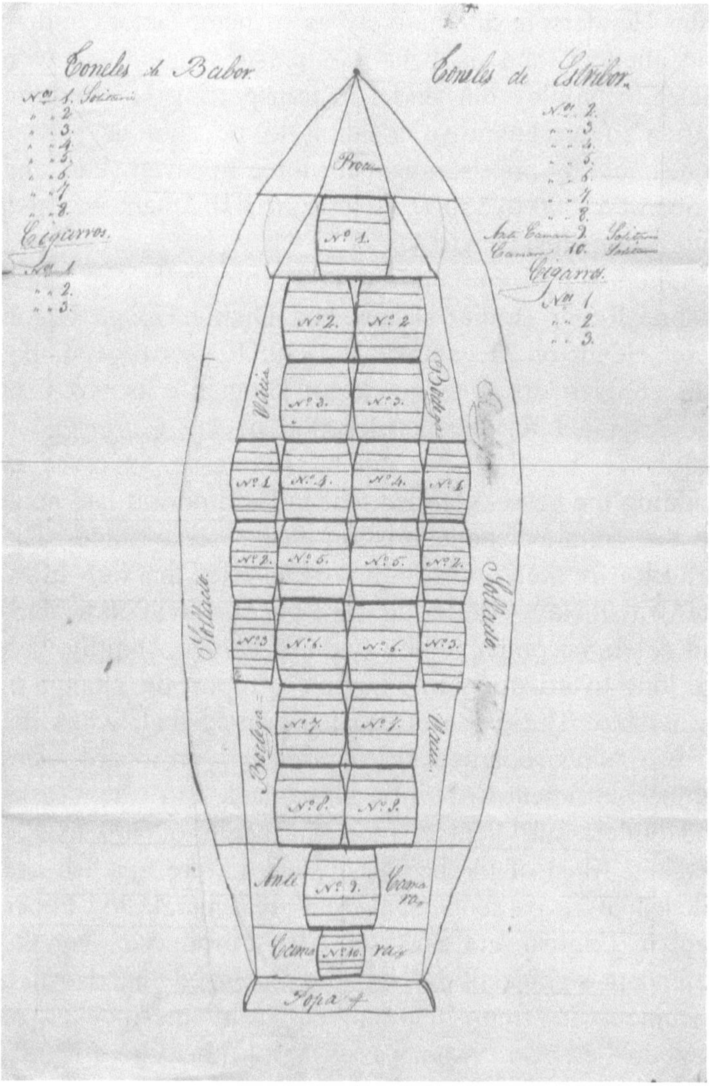

Profile of a Slave Deck found on board the *Catharine*
(*Courtesy National Archives, RG 21, New York*)

23, 1839, ripened into an indictment in six counts under Section 3 of the Act of April 20, 1818, 3 Stat. 450, for fitting out and dispatching the *Catharine*, in concert with John Henderson, alternatively as owners, factors, aiders and abetters, and on behalf of persons unknown, with intent to employ the vessel in transporting blacks from Africa to an unknown location to be sold as slaves, punishable by imprisonment for three to seven years and a fine of $1000 to $5000. A separate indictment was also returned against Henderson.

Allen's trial commenced in Baltimore before Chief Justice Roger Brooke Taney and District Judge Upton Scott Heath on December 4, 1839. It was proved that Allen & Henderson, associates of Thomas Wilson & Co., had arranged for the construction of the *Catharine* in Baltimore, but the Government's witnesses involved in building the vessel claimed that in Baltimore it had none of the fixtures characteristic of the slave trade. The collector for the Port of Baltimore testified that only after the British Navy had brought the *Catharine* to New York did Allen, accompanied by Captain Wedge, comply with the long overdue legal obligation to report the change in ownership. The prosecution also proved that, when the British Navy boarded the *Catharine*, on board were lumber sufficient to build a slave deck and water casks and boilers sufficient to meet the needs of 300 to 400 persons. Most of the people on board were Spanish and alleged to be passengers; there were separate log books kept in English and Spanish. Also introduced over the defendant's objection was an unsigned handwritten document in English, removed from the pocket of Captain Peterson, "who was very lo[a]th to give it up", when the vessel was boarded:

> The main thing for you to do on this voyage is to be ready, in case you are boarded by a man of war, to show your log book, which must be regularly kept from

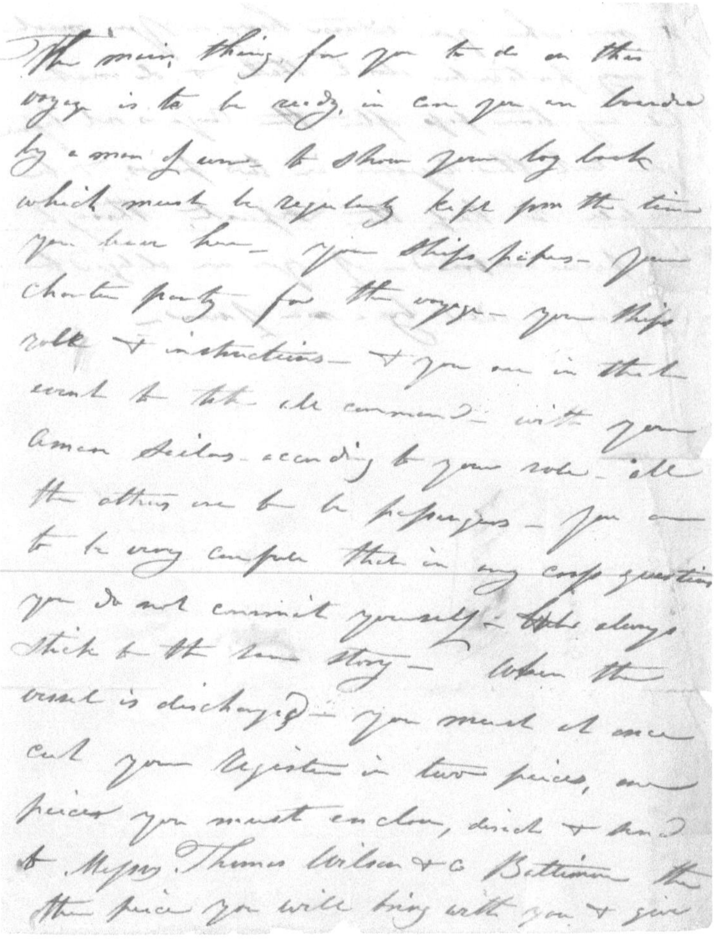

The main thing for you to do on this voyage is to be ready in case you are boarded by a man of war to show your log book which must be regularly kept from the time you leave here—your ships papers—your charter party for the voyage—your ships rolle & instructions—& you are in that event to take all command—with your American sailors according to your role—all the others are to be passengers—You are to be very careful that in any cross questions you do not commit yourself—always stick to the same story—When the vessel is discharged—you must at once cut your Register in two pieces, one piece you must enclose, direct & send to Messrs. Thomas Wilson & Co Baltimore the other piece you will bring with you & give

Unsigned letter seized from Captain Peterson, page 1
(*Courtesy National Archives, RG 21, New York*)

the time you leave here—your ship's papers—your charter party for the voyage—your ship's roll & instructions—& you are in that event to take all command—with your American sailors according to your role—all others are to be passengers—You are to be very careful that in any cross questions you do not commit yourself—always stick to the same story—When the vessel is discharged—you must at once cut

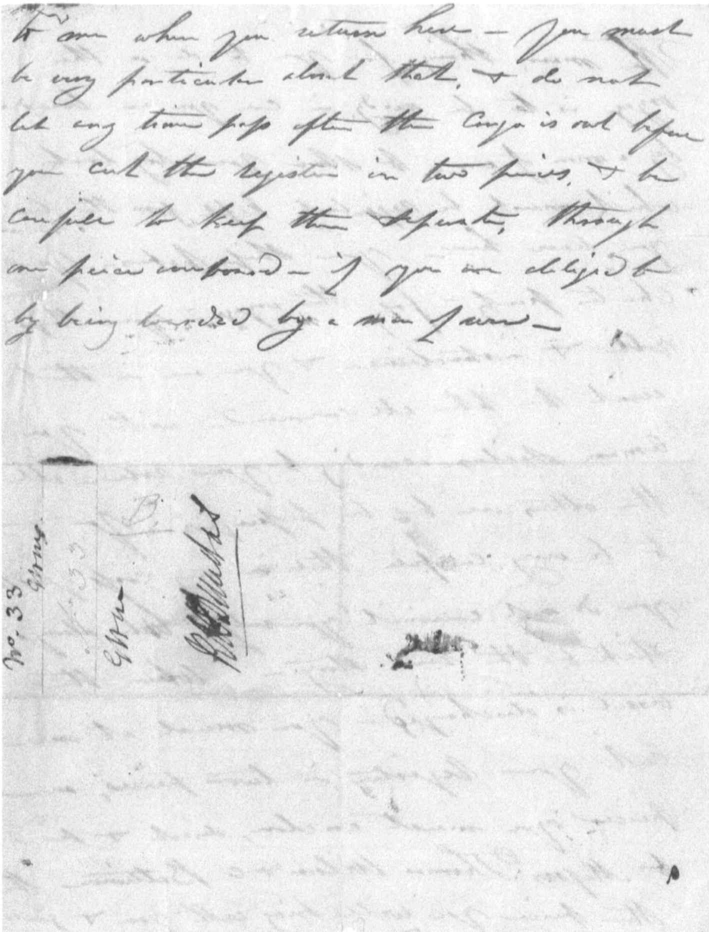
to me when you return here — you must
be very particular about that, & do not
let any time pass after the Cargo is out before
you cut the register in two pieces, & be
careful to keep them separate, through
one piece confound — If you are obliged to
by being boarded by a man of war —

No. 33

Unsigned letter seized from Captain Peterson, page 2
(*Courtesy National Archives, RG 21, New York*)

your register into two pieces, one you must enclose, direct & send to Messrs. Thomas Wilson & Co. Baltimore the other piece you will bring with you & give to me when you return here—you must be very particular about that, & do not let any time pass after the cargo is out before you cut the register in two pieces, & be careful to keep them separate, through

> [sic] one piece overboard—if you are obliged to by being boarded by a man of war—[72]

For the defense, in a deposition Captain Wedge, who had taken the vessel to Havana to sell it, asserted that it was sold through an agent there named Tyng to persons whose names Wedge did not know, and that Wedge had received the sale proceeds but no bill of sale and brought the proceeds back to Baltimore, expecting the consul, with whom he claimed to have left the register, to return it to the collector. On rebuttal, two witnesses from the British Navy testified that Wedge had told them that the *Catharine* had been sold to Pedro Martinez and Co., Dundas adding that it was notorious that Martinez and Co. were "extensive traffi[c]kers in the slave trade."

The Court charged that the vessel did not have to be fully equipped for the trade when sailing from Baltimore for the statute to apply; that if the owners had not intended the vessel to be deployed in the slave trade and if Wedge had made a bona fide sale in Havana with the expectation that the register would be returned to the collector, thereby terminating the *Catharine's* American registry, then Allen could not be convicted even if Wedge had known when he made the sale that the vessel would be so used; but that the fact that the vessel was seized before reaching Africa would not exonerate the owners, if Wedge had been authorized by them to sell the vessel for such a purpose prior to the transfer of title, retaining the protection of the ship's American nationality.

---

[72] The content of this unsigned note is reproduced with minor variations in punctuation and spelling in the report of the British Mixed Commissioners to Lord Palmerston, the *Baltimore Sun* report of the *Allen* trial, Justice Thompson's opinion in the *Catharine*, etc. The version in the text is transcribed from the original document which is in the case file of the *Catharine* in the National Archives.

Not surprisingly, the jury disagreed. The cases of Allen and Henderson were adjourned to the next term of court, in April, so that the consul in Havana, N. P. Trist, could testify concerning the treatment of the register.[73]

United States v. Isaac Morris in the Supreme Court

The Supreme Court made short work of the division of opinion of the circuit court. On February 28, 1840, eleven days after hearing argument from the Attorney General and receiving a written argument from Philip Hamilton, in an opinion by Chief Justice Taney the Supreme Court held unanimously that the statute was applicable to an American serving on a vessel equipped for the slave trade, such as the *Butterfly*, apprehended at a the point in its voyage before its cargo of slaves had been loaded. Citing other federal statutes outside the context of the international slave trade, the Chief Justice said: "To be 'employed' in any thing, means not only the act of doing it, but also to be engaged to do it; to be under contract or orders to do it. And this is not only the ordinary meaning of the word, but it has frequently been

---

[73]*Baltimore Sun,* December 7, 1839, p. 1 and December 10, 1839, p. 1. The newspaper report misstates Wedge's deposition regarding his knowledge of the purchaser. The second news story reports that counsel for Francis Montell also pressed for his trial in connection with the *Butterfly.* No other reference to Montell been located in connection with the *Butterfly.* Presumably counsel was referring to the *Elvira*. See page 62–63, *infra.*

used in that sense in other acts of Congress."[74] The Court construed the Act of May 10, 1800 the same way.[75]

The Forfeiture of the Butterfly

On April 13, 1840, Judge Betts delivered his opinion ordering forfeiture of the *Butterfly*, basing it on several aspects of the evidence before him.[76] He noted that the vessel had sailed from Baltimore with her American

---

[74] 39 U.S. at 475.

[75] It is not without interest that Justice Story's opinion in 1823 in The *Alexander* and Attorney General Gilpin's argument in *Morris* 17 years later, 39 U.S. at 469, both relied on Sir William Scott's opinion in the *Fortuna*, 1 Dodson's Reports 81 (1811), even though Justice Story had earlier concluded in *United States v. The La Jeune Eugenie,* 26 Fed. Cas. 832 (Case No. 15,551)(C.C. D. Mass. 1822), that Scott had departed from it in the later case of the *Le Louis*, 2 Dodson's Reports 210 (1817), a decision adopted by the Supreme Court in The *Antelope,* 23 U.S. 66 (1825). For a brilliant analysis by Richard Henry Dana, Jr., which finds no irreconcilability in the line of British cases in which the *Fortuna* and the *Le Louis* appear, see (Richard Henry Dana, Jr., ed.) Henry Wheaton, *Elements of International Law* (Boston: Little, Brown & Co. 1866), 208–211 n.86.

[76] The opinion is unreported and does not appear in the National Archives file; however, it is reproduced in the *Correspondence with Foreign Powers*, Class D, 102–106. The opinion does not dispose of the claim to the cargo which was lodged by Montero, the supercargo. However, by order dated June 8, 1841, Judge Betts dismissed the claim, evidently on the basis of the argument by the British Government that the issue was one for the Court of Mixed Commission, holding, whether or not Montero be "shown, by competent and satisfactory proof, to be the *bona fide* owner of said property, or entitled at the time the same was seized and captured to its exclusive possession, yet that he was not divested of the possession thereof in such a manner as to be entitled to the interposition of this court to reclaim it from the captors…." *Sessional Papers Printed by Order of the House of Lords, Accounts and Papers,* XIII (1842) Class D, 319–320.

owner as captain, that he was replaced as captain in Havana by the first mate, and that the American crew was replaced by Portuguese and Spanish mariners; otherwise, those on board at the time of capture were the Spanish representative of the entity in Havana which chartered the vessel and fourteen residents of Havana, almost all Spanish, who were listed as passengers. The vessel was furnished with lumber suited for a slave deck and water casks accommodating two to three hundred people. No return cargo for the vessel was stipulated in the charter party, and the vessel was to remain subject to the orders of the charterer without limitation of time at a demurrage lower than the outward voyage.

Judge Betts noted that a similarly equipped vessel flying a Spanish flag would have been subject to seizure under the Anglo-Spanish treaty of 1835 and took judicial notice that "Havana is a port engaged actively in the trade of slaves transported from the coast of Africa." He viewed this evidence as shifting the burden of proof to the claimant and found that the owner had done nothing to establish that this voyage was innocent.

The Second Trial of United States v. Robert W. Allen in Baltimore

Beginning April 18, 1840, Allen was retried on the same indictment in the circuit court in Baltimore before Chief Justice Taney and District Judge Heath. Apart from a reiteration of Wedge's evidence, the principal witness was Nicholas Trist, the American consul in Havana, who, in addition to being subpoenaed in Havana by the prosecution, had been recalled while complaints about his mistreatment in Havana of American mariners and his connivance in the slave trade from Havana were officially investigated.

Nicholas Phillip Trist
(*Courtesy New York Public Library*)

At trial, Trist explained the interactions between his office and the captains of American vessels arriving and clearing Havana. Trist's testimony established that Wedge had observed the legal requirement to deposit his register with the consulate and had obtained the consul's authentication of his transfer to Tyng of his power of attorney from Allen and Henderson. However, according to Trist, Tyng never gave notice to the consulate of his sales of the vessel; when the vessel cleared, the consulate delivered the register to Captain Peterson, whom Tyng had documented at the consulate as the new master of the

Catharine, for a voyage described as follows in the newspaper account:[77]

> [The *Catharine*] sailed from Havana on or about that day [June 28], a charter party having been executed between Tyng and John S. Thrasher, a young man about 21 years of age, connected with his establishment, who was thereby alleged to have contracted for the charter of the vessel....[78]

Apparently the only witnesses called for the defense were character witnesses. The case went to the jury on April 24, and a verdict of acquittal was recorded the following morning. The indictment against Henderson was immediately *nol prossed.*

The Court then proceeded to hear *United States v. Francis T. Montell*, owner of the *Elvira,* which Montell had dispatched in May 1839 to Havana, where the vessel was ostensibly sold by Charles Tyng, who again failed to notify the consulate of the sale; the *Elvira* later returned to Havana from the Gallinas with a cargo of slaves.[79]

---

[77] Baltimore *Sun*, April 25, 1840, page 1. This account states that it is a synopsis, given the full report of the first trial, so it is unclear the extent to which the events surrounding the capture and the contents of the cargo were proved at the second trial.

[78] The newspaper account also states: "There was also a letter of instructions without a signature on board, which directed that the vessel should be delivered up to a Spaniard by the name of Pereira. This letter, it was proved, was in the hand writing of Mr. Tyng." The reporter appears to have conflated, in part, two different documents. The letter with the content he describes does have a purported signature: "J. S. Thrasher". The unsigned letter is the one quoted in full text from the account of the first *Allen* trial. The originals of both are in the *Catharine* case file from the southern district of New York in the National Archives. The handwriting of each is Charles Tyng's. See N. 90, *infra.*

[79] *Baltimore Sun,* April 30, 1840, p.1. This news article summarizes the U. S. district attorney's explanation to the jury in summation of

Montell was charged criminally for engaging in the slave trade and separately sued for failing to comply with the legal requirement to return the register to the collector in Baltimore; his defense was that the sale was bona fide and he had not sanctioned any of the acts that followed. The absence of proof of his authorization of the conduct following the sale and his high standing in the community led to his acquittal on the criminal charge[80] by the jury "in a few minutes".[81]

---

the reason for that slavers held onto their American register and displayed the American flag on their outwards voyages from Havana to the African coast:

> It was also explained to the jury why it was that the slave dealers were so anxious to preserve their American character until they arrived on the coast of Africa, and on that account to have the register on board. By a treaty between England, Spain and Portugal, a right was granted to British cruizers to examine vessels under those flags on the coast of Africa, and if fitted for slavers or engaged in the traffic, they were taken before a mixed tribunal, either at Sierra Leone, Havana or Bahia, and if the vessels were condemned they were broken up. But the American government would not permit the right to search American vessels, and Americans offending against the laws against the slave trade, could be tried only by American tribunals; consequently one half of the hazardous voyage was deprived of its risk if a vessel could reach the coast of Africa under American colors, commanded by an American, and with an American register.

[80] However, Montell was found liable for $1200.00 on his bond for failure to return the register to the collector as required by Section 7 of the Act of December 31, 1792. *United States v. Montell*, 26 Fed. Cas. 1293 (Case No. 15,798) (C.C.D.Md. 1841)(Taney, Ch.J.) The judgment in an earlier action on a $400.00 bond under Section 1 of the Act of February 28, 1803 (2 Stat. 203), relating to seamen aboard, had been reversed by Chief Justice Taney. *Montell v. United States,* 17 Fed. Cas. 612 (Case No. 9723) (C.C.D.Md. 1840).

[81] Trist proceeded to Washington, where he called on John Quincy Adams on the afternoon of May 8. According to the entry in Adams's diary:

> Mr. Trist, Consul of the United States at the Havanna, was here this morning and I had a long conversation with him upon the

The Catharine

Forfeiture Proceedings in the District Court (S.D.N.Y.)

The United States district attorney, Benjamin F. Butler, commenced forfeiture proceedings against the *Catharine* on December 30, 1839, alleging in multiple

---

charges against his official conduct which are now under consideration by the Committee of Commerce of the House of Representatives. The charges are of two kinds: first, by several masters of vessels complaining of abusive official ill treatment of them; and, secondly, of his gross and culpable connivance at the African slave-trade carried on from the United States, chiefly from Baltimore, through the Havana. I had received two letters from him urging me to bring the matter forward in the House of Representatives; and assigned now to him my reasons for declining to do this – the chief of which was... his solemn protestations of innocence, and his undoubting confidence of proving it.... He has just now returned from Baltimore where he has been as a witness upon two trials for slave trade cases, in both of which the defendants were acquitted – in both, he says, undoubtedly guilty. I suppose it is as impossible to convict a slave trader at Baltimore as in the Island of Cuba, and I fear Mr. Trist's defence rests on the same basis as that of the late defendants at Baltimore – the inexecutability of the law. He told me that no man's life would be safe who would attempt to execute the law at the Havana.

Adams was being disingenuous to Trist. A month earlier, according to his diary, he had forced his way into the State Department and read Trist's correspondence:

> The morning was devoted principally to the perusal of the dispatches from N.P. Trist, Consul of the United States at the Havanna, concerning the fraudulent use of the flag of the United States for carrying on the African slave-trade. They are voluminous, and manifest either the vilest treachery or the most culpable indifference to his duties. For the last three years...there has been the most shameful prostitution of the American flag to carry on that traffic...openly notoriously practised before his face; [and] that as Consul for the United States, and at the same time Acting Consul for Portugal, he has actively lent his aid to it...

Charles Francis Adams (ed.), *Memoirs of John Quincy Adams, Comprising Portions of His Diary from 1795 To 1848* (Philadelphia: Lippincott, 1876), X, 255, 283–284.

counts under three statutes that the vessel was forfeit because, for use in the slave trade, the vessel was built in Baltimore, sailed to Havana and sold, and from there was proceeding to the African coast when captured. Judge Betts would later note in his opinion that the trial concerned only the fifth count, which charged that on July 1, 1839—at sea on the way to Africa—the *Catharine* was "employed or made use of" in the carrying of slaves from one country to another by persons who were either citizens or residents of the United States, in violation of the Act of May 10, 1800.[82]

There were two kinds of claimants also participating in the proceeding: two individuals who had been part of the crew, sailing under assumed names to appear American but who were not and who were sent with the vessel to New York, and Charles Tyng, identifying himself as an American born in Newburyport where he resided until moving to Havana in 1837, a "shipbroker and commission agent" by profession, claiming to be the owner of the *Catharine*. The first two, William Michael and James Foxcroft, asserted their ignorance of any intended employment of the *Catharine* in the slave trade, although Foxcroft did admit that on the voyage he was employed in making "sennett", a kind of rope, which he was told would be used to bind slaves and which was produced in far greater quantities than the ship would otherwise have need for.

Tyng's claim, however, would make a good script for an Italian comic opera if its purpose were not so nefarious. According to Tyng's written pleading,[83] the

---

[82] *United States v. The Catharine,* 25 Fed. Cas. 332, 336 (Case No. 14,755)(S.D.N.Y. 1840).

[83] The files for both the *Butterfly* and the *Catharine* in the National Archives are very curious. The files for the *Catharine* contain some of the original documents seized from aboard the vessel by the British Navy, depositions of Foxcroft and some of the naval

Catharine came to Havana from Baltimore in May, 1839, under the command of William Wedge, who had a power of attorney from its owners, R. W. Allen and John Henderson, to sell the vessel; he was also authorized by the power of attorney to grant his powers thereunder to others. Tyng arranged a sale of the *Catharine* to Don Pedro Martinez & Co. in early June, 1839, for $7,750, delivering the vessel the day after the terms of sale had been agreed and before payment had been made, confident that the transaction would be consummated by the exchange of title for payment of the agreed sales price. At that point, according to Tyng, the "principal member" of Martinez & Co. who had negotiated the purchase was called away to Matanzas on other business, and Wedge discovered that there was a vessel about to leave for Philadelphia which he wanted passage on. So confident was Tyng that the sale would close, his claim asserts, based on "great wealth and respectable standing" of Pedro Martinez & Co., that he advanced the purchase price to Wedge to take back to Baltimore, before Martinez had paid a penny, and Wedge, in turn, vested in Tyng his full authority to dispose of the *Catharine* under the power of attorney. While the unnamed "principal member" of Martinez & Co. was still in Matanzas, Tyng

---

personnel who sailed the vessel to New York, and correspondence between the United States district attorneys in the districts of Maryland and the southern district of New York regarding the cases. On the other hand, although the files for both vessels appear to contain the original orders made in the district court, the other original court papers from the district court are not to be found there; the texts of those are recoverable only from the "apostles", the old-fashioned word applied to the record on appeal in admiralty cases. In the related case of *Allen v. United States,* 1 Fed. Cas. 518, 519 (Case No. 240) (C.C.D.Md. 1840), it is stated that "Ting's" pleading in the *Catharine* was filed on March 27, 1840.

For purposes of this narrative, the written pleading reproduced in the apostle is fuller that the statement of the case reproduced from Paine's *Reports* in *Federal Cases.*

was approached by "another member of the said firm", also unnamed, who, on June 15, 1839, effected through Tyng a one-way charter of the vessel to the island of Principe, off the African coast, to John S. Thrasher, described in the claim simply as "an American citizen residing in Havana" but proven at the second *Allen* trial in Baltimore to be a 21-year-old clerical employee of Tyng's.[84]

---

[84] When a man of more mature years, Thrasher proved to be as much trouble as his employer, Tyng; indeed, the two became business partners. In late 1851 the Cuban authorities arrested Thrasher for treason for statements he published in the Havana *Faro Industrial,* summarily tried him for treason and sentenced him to eight years imprisonment at hard labor in the quicksilver mines in Ceuta, Africa; he was immediately deported to Spain. However, the intervention of the local American authorities and Secretary of State Daniel Webster, relying on his United States citizenship to negate any duty to the Spanish Crown punishable in the breach as treason, coupled with assistance from Tyng, led to his pardon while still in Spain in transit. *Message of the President of the United States Transmitting Information respecting the imprisonment, &c., of John S. Thrasher*, 32d Cong., 1st Sess. (Dec. 23, 1851); *Message of the President of the United States Transmitting Further Information respecting the imprisonment, &c., of John S. Thrasher*, 32d Cong., 1st Sess., (Jan. 2, 1852); *Works of Daniel Webster* (Boston: Little, Brown & Co. 1853), Vol. 6, 518–530; *Case of the Black Warrior, and other Violations of the Rights of American Citizens by Spanish Authorities* (Washington, Senate Printer 1854), 107–129. Later, Thrasher participated in the filibustering activities of John A. Quitman in 1854, posting bail by order of Associate Justice John A. Campbell, and carried on a prominent career as a journalist in the Confederates States during the Civil War. J.F.H. Claiborne, *Life and Correspondence of John A. Quitman* (New York: Harper & Bros. 1860), Vol. 2, 196–209; *United States v. Quitman,* 27 Fed. Cas. 680 (Case No. 16,111) (C.C.E.D.La. 1854); Janice Ruth Wood, "John S. Thrasher: Journalistic Revolutionary and Reformer", in (Patricia G. McNeely et al., eds.), *Knights of the Quill:Confederate Correspondents and their Civil War Reporting* (West Lafayette, Ind.: Purdue Univ. Press 2010), 362.

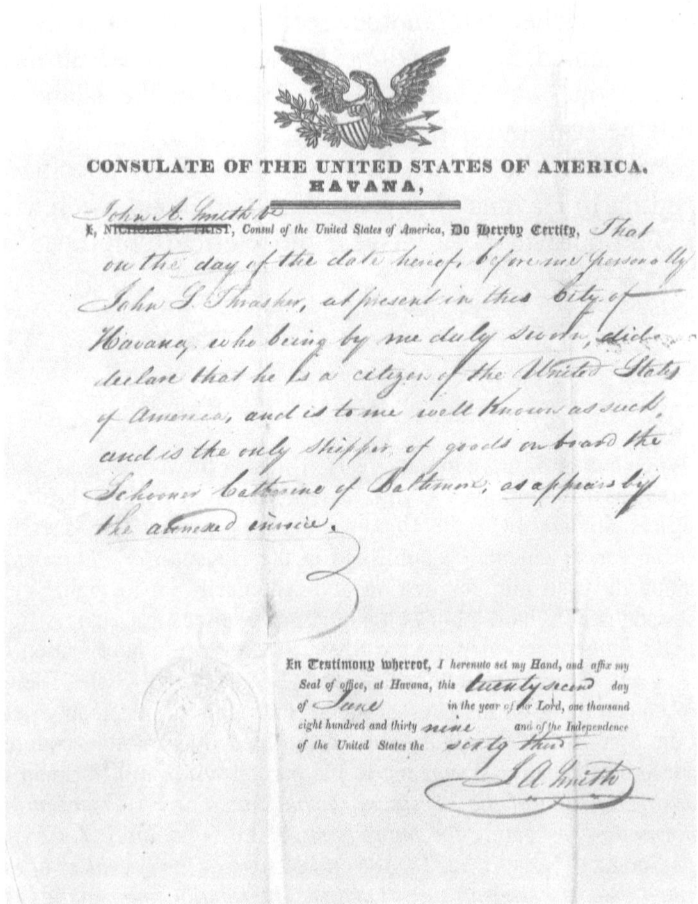

CONSULATE OF THE UNITED STATES OF AMERICA.
HAVANA,

John A. Smith ~~I, NICHOLAS P. TRIST~~, Consul of the United States of America, Do Hereby Certify, That on the day of the date hereof, before me personally John G. Thrasher, at present in this City of Havana, who being by me duly sworn, did declare that he is a citizen of the United States of America, and is to me well known as such, and is the only shipper of goods on board the Schooner Catharine of Baltimore, as appears by the annexed invoice.

In Testimony whereof, I hereunto set my Hand, and affix my Seal of office, at Havana, this twenty second day of June in the year of our Lord, one thousand eight hundred and thirty nine and of the Independence of the United States the sixty third.

J. A. Smith

Consular certificate for Thrasher
(Courtesy National Archives, RG 21, New York)

The "principal member" of Pedro Martinez & Co. returned to Havana after ten days away, and Tyng sent in a bill for the purchase price of the *Catharine*. Claiming that the *Catharine* lacked the heavy coppering represented during negotiations, Pedro Martinez & Co. refused to close the transaction. Concluding that a lawsuit in Havana would be "exceedingly dilatory and expensive", Tyng was fortunate to find another buyer, one Simon Perez de Teran, with whom he signed a contract on June

25, 1839 for $10,000.00: Teran agreed to pay $7,500.00 immediately and the balance on delivery of the vessel to Bona on the African coast, subject to the prior charter of John S. Thrasher, who accommodated the transaction by limiting his rights under the charter party after discharge of the outbound cargo to permit timely delivery to the pur-

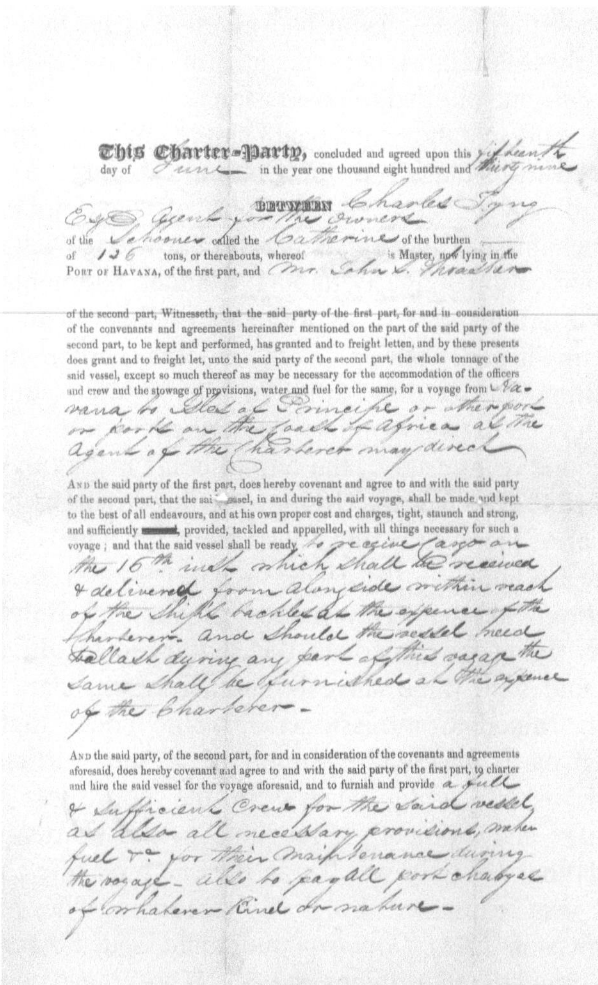

This Charter-Party, concluded and agreed upon this fifteenth day of June in the year one thousand eight hundred and thirty nine

BETWEEN Charles Tyng Esq Agent for the Owners of the Schooner called the Catherine of the burthen of 126 tons, or thereabouts, whereof is Master, now lying in the PORT OF HAVANA, of the first part, and Mr. John S. Thrasher

of the second part, Witnesseth, that the said party of the first part, for and in consideration of the convenants and agreements hereinafter mentioned on the part of the said party of the second part, to be kept and performed, has granted and to freight letten, and by these presents does grant and to freight let, unto the said party of the second part, the whole tonnage of the said vessel, except so much thereof as may be necessary for the accommodation of the officers and crew and the stowage of provisions, water and fuel for the same, for a voyage from Havana to Isles of Principe or other port or ports on the Coast of Africa as the Agent of the Charterer may direct

AND the said party of the first part, does hereby covenant and agree to and with the said party of the second part, that the sai[d ve]ssel, in and during the said voyage, shall be made and kept to the best of all endeavours, and at his own proper cost and charges, tight, staunch and strong, and sufficiently [redacted], provided, tackled and apparelled, with all things necessary for such a voyage; and that the said vessel shall be ready to receive Cargo on the 16th inst which shall be received & delivered from alongside within reach of the Ship's tackles at the expence of the Charterer. And should the vessel need Ballast during any part of this voyage the same shall be furnished at the expence of the Charterer -

AND the said party, of the second part, for and in consideration of the covenants and agreements aforesaid, does hereby covenant and agree to and with the said party of the first part, to charter and hire the said vessel for the voyage aforesaid, and to furnish and provide a full & sufficient Crew for the said vessel, as also all necessary provisions, water fuel &c for their maintenance during the voyage - also to pay all port charges of whatever kind or nature -

First page of Thrasher charter party
(*Courtesy National Archives, RG 21, New York*)

chaser elsewhere in Africa pursuant to an addendum to the charter party of even date.

The final blow, according to Charles Tyng, was, of course, the capture of the *Catharine* by the *Dolphin.* Teran refused to pay the balance due under the contract and brought suit against Tyng in Havana to recover the money he had advanced. Allen and Henderson refused to pay back the money Tyng had given Wedge. In Tyng's view, these circumstances made him the owner of the *Catharine* and entitled to possession.

Of course, the contrived nature of this farce—designed to insulate both the Baltimore builders and the outward voyage from accusations of slave trading—becomes immediately apparent with knowledge that there is no indication Judge Betts had. Madden had unmasked Pedro Martinez & Co. as a leader of the Cuban slave trade in his deposition eight months earlier in his deposition in *Amistad* trial in the district court in Connecticut; it was similarly described in testimony in the second *Allen* trial in the circuit court in Baltimore in April 1840. On April 4, 1840, over three months before the trial of the case before Judge Betts on July 10, 1840, off the Gallinas the British Navy had captured the *Eliza Davidson,* another Havana-based ship of Baltimore origins flying the American flag, equipped for the slave trade and with three slave boys already on board. The British Mixed Commissioners' report noted that the charter party was with "Simon de Teran, sufficiently known as a leading partner in the house of Pedro Martinez and Company"; recourse to the charter party reveals that not only was Teran the charterer, the charter party was witnessed by J. S. Thrasher. The Mixed Commission *Eliza Davidson* judgment, dated April 18, 1840, among other things states: "The Havana laders, consignees, and supposed owners of the cargo are the same Cuba merchants, Simon de Teran and Charles Tyng, who appeared so recently in this court in the cases of the '*Asp*' and '*Lark*'; and the former is not only the professed charterer, but, as appears by the tenor of the charter-party which declares him to be so, is connected with the vessel in a still more intimate relation, and is indeed virtually her owner." In their report of March 18, 1840, in the case of the *Asp*, the British Mixed Commissioners referred to Tyng by name as "agent for the vessel and shipper of the cargo, the better to keep a name so notorious as Martinez and Co. out of view..." [85] As previously noted, Tyng was the central figure in yet another, virtually identical transaction in the case against Montell tried in Baltimore at the end of April. Finally, as also noted, Thrasher—the purported charterer of the *Catharine*, on whose behalf another unnamed member of Martinez and Co. allegedly approached Tyng during the brief period before the firm repudiated its purchase of the *Catharine*, substituting one of its "leading partners"—turns out to be a 21-year-old clerk in Tyng's office.[86]

Judge Betts recognized in his opinion "that this whole arrangement bears the semblance of being a common concern between Thrasher and Teran ... that the vessel should wear her American character to the coast of Africa, with a view probably to avoid the application of the treaty between England and Spain, and the hazard of interception by English cruisers; and that when there, she should become Spanish, before venturing on her return voyage, lest the officers and crew might be declared pirates under the act of Congress of May 15, 1820". Tyng's involvement makes clear that, from beginning to end, the *Catharine* was intended for the slave trade. However, apparently uninformed of the known breadth of

---

[85] *Correspondence with the British Commissioners,* Class A, 28–29, 73–76.

[86] Robert E. May, *Manifest Destiny's Underworld – Filibustering in Antebellum America* (UNC 2002), 229.

Tyng's activities and employment of Thrasher, Judge Betts left Tyng out of his analysis. As a result, the judge seems to have viewed the outward voyage under the Thrasher charter as breaking the chain of causation with the outfitting of the *Catharine* for the slave trade in Havana, with the proof of which he was satisfied, and the subsequent delivery to Teran at another African port, for a return voyage under the Spanish flag. For the Act of May 10, 1800 to apply, according to Judge Betts:

> But it is apprehended a prosecution under the first section against the vessel, cannot be sustained without showing that the whole adventure contemplated by her, is to be performed by her in her American character....There is nothing in this statute to reach an American vessel built and fitted out for the slave trade, but actually sold to a foreigner and employed by him.... No evidence was offered...nor other fact evincing the object of the voyage to be continuous and identical.... I am accordingly bound to hold, upon the testimony, that the vessel sailed from Havana to deliver a cargo at Principe, and was then wholly discharged and separated from that employment, and was after that to be taken to Bona, and delivered to the purchaser."[87]

Accordingly, on August 4, 1840, Judge Betts dismissed the libel against the *Catharine*, decreeing that the vessel was not engaged in the slave trade as an American vessel when seized. On August 12, the United States district attorney appealed to the circuit court.

---

[87] 25 Fed. Cas. at 337.

The Trial of Isaac Morris in the Circuit Court (S.D.N.Y.)

Part Two

The circuit court docket book reflects that the trial of Isaac Morris resumed on July 30, 1840 before Judge Betts, sitting alone, with one juror absent. No report of the content of the trial proceedings has been located. *Niles National Register* for August 8, 1840, reports Morris's conviction. A motion in arrest of judgment was made on August 10th and denied on the 12th, when Morris received the maximum sentence of 2 years imprisonment and a two thousand dollar fine.

Evidently Morris was still on bail following the sentence, because an entry in the docket book for December 24, 1840 shows that his bail was forfeited. This suggests that he absconded; further information has not been located.[88]

Allen v. United States

Action on the Bond (D.Md.) under the Act of 1792

As was the case with Montell, Allen and Henderson, along with Wedge—having posted a bond pursuant to

---

[88] There is no record of any proceedings on the indictment against Peterson, captain of the *Catharine,* nor has any explanation of that circumstance been located. However, the report of the *Dolphin* concerning the capture of the *Catharine* states that "Peterson...evidently is neither English nor American... probably a German or a Swede." *Correspondence with the British Commissioners,* Class A, 98. It is likely, therefore, that the statute under which he was indicted did not apply to him, being neither a U.S. citizen or resident, and the indictment was dismissed.

Section 7 of the Act of December 31, 1792, securing their obligation to deliver to the collector of the port of Baltimore the register of the *Catharine* upon its sale to a foreign owner—were sued on the bond in the district court in Baltimore on October 12, 1839, for their failure to do so and found liable after trial in the March term, 1840. The district court rejected their proffer of the record of the proceedings in the *Catharine* before Judge Betts as proof that the *Catharine* was not purchased by a foreigner in Havana, based on "Ting's" claim there that he was the owner. By the time their appeal reached Chief Justice Taney in the November 1840 term of the circuit court, Judge Betts had held that the *Catharine* was not a vessel of the United States engaged in the slave trade at the time of detention by the British Navy. The Chief Justice rejected the argument that Judge Betts's ruling was dispositive both of the nationality of the vessel as well as the use to which the *Catharine* being put at the time, holding that Judge Betts's judgment was equally open to the construction that the *Catharine* was employed in the slave trade at the time of seizure but not as a vessel of the United States; it did not necessarily establish ownership or nationality. Moreover, the Chief Justice held, in an action for a penalty involving other parties, the judgment in an admiralty case could not be preclusive as a matter of law. The judgment on the bond was affirmed.[89]

The Catharine *Condemned in the Circuit Court (S.D.N.Y.)*

During Christmas week 1840 U.S. Supreme Court Justice Smith Thompson was in New York City holding

---

[89] 1 Fed. Cas. at 520.

the circuit court. According to the docket book, on December 21 he heard argument on the appeal brought by Hamilton from Judge Betts's decree forfeiting the *Butterfly*, and on December 23 affirmed the forfeiture. On December 24 he heard oral argument on Butler's appeal from Judge Betts's dismissal of the forfeiture proceedings against the *Catharine* and reversed that decision. Formal decrees were made on January 20, 1841 and signed in February, 1841.

In reaching his conclusion in the *Catharine*, Justice Thompson disagreed with Judge Betts's apparent construction of the statute to require that the slave-trading portion of the voyage needed to be done as an American vessel. Instead, in addition to the facts identified by Judge Betts as tending to show that, once under a different flag on the African coast, it was intended that the vessel be used in the slave trade, Justice Thompson marshaled the additional evidence that the cargo being shipped—the lumber, the leagers, and the boilers, as well as the 350 pairs of manacles first found after the decree in the district court and entered in the record in the circuit court—were suited for the conversion of the *Catharine* into a slave ship. To this he added the unsigned letter of instructions the British naval officers wrested from Captain Peterson and the letter to Peterson, signed with Thrasher's name, directing him, once at the Island of Principe, to consign the vessel and its cargo to Pereya, the supercargo on the outward voyage who committed suicide on arrival in New York in British custody.[90] In

[90] Tyng's formal hand in his correspondence in the Caleb Cushing Papers in the Library of Congress—seeking to be appointed Consul in Havana in his February 5, 1853 letter, for example—appears the same as the hand in the Thrasher letter to Captain Peterson dated June 28, 1839. The authentication of the unsigned letter of instructions wrested from Peterson when the *Catharine* was boarded as also in Tyng's handwriting at the second *Allen* trial is confirmed

conclusion, "if there was a concerted plan," as Judge Betts had found, between Thrasher and Teran, "the more easily to elude capture and condemnation": [91]

> [I]t is difficult to conceive how Tyng, the claimant, could have been ignorant of the object and purpose for which the arrangement was made, and he must, therefore, be considered a party to it, and the whole must be taken to be one continuous enterprise; and, if so, the mere change of property in the vessel after her arrival on the coast of Africa, could not legalize the transaction. The penalty incurred, and the forfeiture attached from the very inception of the voyage, if it was commenced for the purpose of taking on board and transporting slaves. It is true that the penalty of this act of congress is leveled against American property employed in the manner prohibited. But I cannot think that the confiscation is limited to the American interest at the time she is engaged in the actual transportation of slaves.[92]

---

by comparison with undisputed exemplars found in the on-line Cushing papers and with a page of the manuscript reproduced (at viii) in Tyng's published partial autobiography, *Before the Wind: The Memoir of an American Sea Captain, 1808–1833* (New York: Viking 1999). The concluding statement of the editor of that book, said to be his great great grandaughter: "Although we might wish that Charles Tyng had completed the written account of his life, it seems likely that the years he describes in his memoir were the most adventurous and dramatic" needs to be re-evaluated with knowledge of his activities in Havana during the period there omitted but reflected in these pages, as does his apparently positive designation by Phillips Academy as a "noteworthy alumnus" in its class of 1811 (https://www.andover.edu/About/NotableAlumni/LongList/Pages/1800.aspx), last visited January 26, 2016.

[91] 25 Fed. Cas. at 336.

[92] 25 Fed. Cas. at 341. Nevertheless, by order of Justice Thompson and Judge Betts in the circuit court on January 4, 1842, the wage claims of William Michael and James Foxcroft were allowed from the proceeds of the sale of the *Catharine*.

The *Catharine* circuit court case file contains an undated "appeal" to the Supreme Court, signed by counsel for Tyng. There is no indication that the appeal was prosecuted, and *The Law Reporter* for April, 1844, contains the following entry for the Supreme Court of the United States on March 9, 1844:[93]

> No. 22 Charles Tyng, claimant of the schooner Catharine v. the United States. This appeal from the circuit court of the United States for New York was, by consent of counsel, dismissed.

---

[93] *The Law Reporter* (April, 1844) 558.

PART II

WARREN HOWARD'S CRITICISMS

WARREN HOWARD'S CRITICISMS

Howard attacks Judge Betts's jurisprudence in two instances: first, at the *Morris* criminal trial, in failing to follow Justice Story's analysis in the *Alexander* and instead questioning whether slaves needed to be on the *Butterfly* at the time of capture to trigger a statute applicable to a vessel "engaged in the transportation of slaves"; and second, in dismissing the forfeiture proceeding against the *Catharine,* treating the pretextual voyage to the African coast under the Thrasher charter party as separate from the intended return voyage to Havana with the cargo of slaves for which the ship—even before the discovery of 350 pairs of handcuffs in the hold—was quite obviously equipped. The former Howard dismisses as "pettifoggery", and the latter he describes as reversed by Justice Thompson because of "the stupidity of Betts's reasoning." Betts "still did not grasp the essential point of the Supreme Court's rulings: a vessel was engaged in the slave trade as soon as she was destined for it..."[94] A response to these criticisms is deferred for a moment, in order to contextualize Judge Betts's ultimately inconsequential but entirely legitimate moments of doubt in these cases with related far greater political myopia (at best) of the United States and relevant errors of law by others in high places, both

---

[94] Howard, 162–163.

intentional and otherwise, leading to their filing in the southern district of New York.

First and foremost, the fault lies with the government of the United States. The Executive Branch and the Senate between them thwarted every effort by Great Britain, at least one on the verge of success, to make prohibition of the international slave trade effective by enlisting the United States to participate in the web of bilateral treaties permitting mutual search, repeatedly promoted by Great Britain to eradicate the international slave trade in the some twenty years prior to August, 1839. The United States preferred to keep fighting the War of 1812, rather than help to eradicate the international slave trade.

Second, the Van Buren administration supported the slave interests of Spain in the *Amistad* proceedings in the district of Connecticut and the Supreme Court of the United States in the face of admitted violation of Spain's own laws and its international treaty obligations.

Third, the British Navy's searches and seizures of the *Butterfly* and the *Catharine* were undoubtedly in violation of international law. Each was flying the American flag when accosted. Nothing in particular suggested that either was engaged in the slave trade before their boarding by naval personnel. The distinction made by Lord Ashburton that such conduct was merely a "visitation" to check the vessel's credentials, rather than a search, had no legal basis. Richard Henry Dana, Jr.'s lucid summary of the law in his revision of *Wheaton* makes the point:

> There is no case to be found in which an English court of the last resort has directly decided, that, in time of peace, when there was no color of belligerent right, a British cruiser could search a foreign vessel on the ground of suspicion of being a slaver....No case has been found where, either in England or the United

> States, a distinction has been sustained by the court between a right of visit and a right of search.[95]

That said, the leading historian of the Cuban slave trade has rightly emphasized "...the central point that British antislavery policy was most successful when it was most illegal. The treaty systems and naval initiatives that remained on the right side of international law would not, by themselves, have ended the slave trade."[96]

Fourth, if, in August 1839, when the *Butterfly* and the *Catharine* were seized by the British Navy, the Mixed Commission in Freetown, Sierra Leone, had not persisted in its blanket refusal to take jurisdiction of any vessel seized by the British Navy while flying American colors and had instead been willing to look at the totality of the evidence of nationality– as it should have done and began to do after receiving Lord Palmerston's report of the Queen's Advocate-General's opinion on the subject in late 1839—there would have been no need to send the *Butterfly* and the *Catharine* to the southern district of New York for forfeiture proceedings.

Fifth, after the vessels' arrival in New York, both the Queen's Advocate-General and the United States district attorney for the Southern District of New York incorrectly concluded that legally such proceedings would fail. The Queen's Advocate-General informed Lord Palmerston that the *Butterfly* and the *Catharine* were not subject to forfeiture under the laws of the United States, and Palmerston, in turn, told the British Consul in

---

[95] *Elements of International Law,* 213–214, n.89. A treaty could alter this rule between the contracting parties, but Dana painstakingly shows that all efforts to establish a mutual right of search between Great Britain and America by treaty failed. *Ibid.,* 201–203 n.85.

[96] David Eltis, "Was Abolition of the U.S. and British Slave Trade Significant in the Broader Atlantic Context?", 66 (2009) *William and Mary Quarterly* 717, 731–32 n.16.

New York to accept no more such ships from the Navy. Benjamin F. Butler had refused to proceed against two similarly situated vessels, the *Eagle* and the *Clara* and, despite Justice Story's opinion, believed that the Act of 1800 was inapplicable to such vessels.

It should be plain from this recital that these ships need never have been sent to New York and could have been proceeded against in the Mixed Commission in Sierra Leone, provided one turns a blind eye to Great Britain's violations of international law in seizing them to begin with. It is equally plain that respectable lawyers in high positions in both countries had doubts about the legal viability of forfeiture proceedings against the *Butterfly* and the *Catharine* in the southern district of New York.

Finally, as earlier demonstrated, far more compelling proof was available to the United States district attorney in the *Catharine* than was ever offered to the Court. In the *Morris* case, the newspaper report of the proceedings on November 30, 1839, quoted above, suggest less a disagreement between Judge Betts and Justice Thompson, whom Howard deservedly treats as a fine, anti-slavery judge, than an opinion shared by those two judges at odds with Justice Story's in the *Alexander* and a wish to have the issue settled by the Supreme Court by the device of a certificate of division. However, if Judge Betts was wrong in his apparent view in the *Morris* case that, to succeed, the prosecution had to prove that there were slaves on board at the time of the vessel's capture, he was hardly the first eminent government official to make a mistake in the legal saga of these two vessels.

Judge Betts's "Pettifoggery"

Relying on its prior construction of unrelated statutes with similar language, the Supreme Court ruled, unanimously, in *United States v. Isaac Morris* that the Act of 1800 applied to the *Butterfly*, whether loaded with slaves or not. But "pettifoggery"—that is, "under-handed", "disreputable" or "quibbling about petty points"? This accusation needs to be considered in the context of discussion of Britain's treaties with Portugal and Spain, which from their origins had required slaves on board to justify British naval intervention, and only in 1835, four years earlier, had been expanded to add an "equipment clause" to the Spanish treaty only. The Portuguese never agreed to such an extension of their treaty arrangements, with the result that the British Parliament unilaterally, and in violation of international law, authorized British cruisers to seize Portuguese vessels equipped for the slave trade without slaves aboard. And, of course, Great Britain and the United States had no treaty at all.

The Queen Against Serva and Nine Others
(*December 11, 1845*)

More instructive still is a slightly later case involving the slave trade, heard in Great Britain before all but two of the common law judges in commission, including the Chief Justices of all three common law courts. The case arose in late February, 1845 from the boarding off the coast of Africa and subsequent detention of a Brazilian ship, the *Felicidade,* by a British naval vessel, the H.M.S. *Wasp;* the *Felicidade* was equipped for the slave trade but had no slaves aboard. With most of the *Felicidade's* Brazilian crew removed to the *Wasp* and sixteen British sailors aboard, the *Felicidade* was sent in pursuit of another Brazilian vessel, the *Echo.* The chase ended a day later with the capture of the *Echo,* which was found to have 434 slaves then aboard. The *Echo's* captain, Serva, and a dozen of its crew were transferred to the *Felicidade,* of which a British midshipman and nine British sailors were left in charge. Within an hour Serva and his shipmates, led by the *Felicidade's* cook, rose against their British captors, murdered all ten of them, and sailed away in the *Felicidade*.

They were pursued, apprehended, indicted and put on trial at the Exeter Assizes in late July, 1845, for the murder of the British midshipman in command, whom the cook had stabbed in the side with a long cooking knife, grabbed by the feet and thrown overboard.[97] Three were acquitted, and seven were convicted and sentenced to death. Among the witnesses called by the prosecution was the captain of the *Felicidade,* who testified that his ship was on its way to Africa to pick up a cargo of slaves when apprehended by the *Wasp.* The defense claimed at trial, and later successfully on appeal, that, nevertheless, the defendants were entitled to acquittal because, in the absence of slaves on board, the *Wasp's* seizure of the *Felicidade* had been illegal, and that factual circumstances arising from it tainted both the *Felicidade's* capture of the *Echo* and the subsequent detention of Serva and some of its crew on the *Felicidade,* and justified their murder of ten British seamen as an act of self-defense.

---

[97] According to the trial testimony, another "of the Englishmen was thrown partly overboard, and hung by the side of the vessel—this was the sentry; he had caught hold of the fore-sheet and held to it; Antonio Joaquim then went to him and cut his fingers off, and he sank into the water and disappeared."

After some initial resistance on his part, the trial judge stated a case for review by the legally informal but centuries-old conference of the "twelve judges" of the King's Bench, Common Pleas and Exchequer, now with an authorized strength of fifteen and three years away from being codified by statute in 1848 as the Court for Crown Cases Reserved. [98] Decisions by the judges were—as in *Serva*—often not accompanied by formal opinions and were effected in the court from which the case had been certified. Lord Chief Justice Denman—who sat in *Serva* with the Lord Chief Justice of Common Pleas and the Lord Chief Baron of the Exchequer and ten of their colleagues, and whose dissatisfaction with the result led him to propose the codification of the existence of what he called "The Court of all the Judges"—described it this way:

> This Court is a voluntary meeting of all the Judges, without commission or mandate, without seconds or officers. It has met and consulted from an early period of our history to determine questions of importance. Many of the cases reported by Lord Coke were finally decided there. The judgment, indeed, was pronounced in that Court to which the record belonged; but it is believed to have been always conformable to the conclusion at which the assembled Judges, or the majority of them, had arrived. The meetings were held in the apartment called the Exchequer Chamber, but were never called by that name and style, which,

---

[98] James Oldham, "Informal Lawmaking in England by the Twelve Judges in the Late Eighteenth and Early Nineteenth Centuries", 29 (2011) *Law and History Review*, 181; D.R. Bentley (ed.), *Select Cases from the Twelve Judges' Notebooks* (London: J. Rees, 1997), 13–14. Professor Oldham's focus is on a slightly earlier period than *Serva.*

> indeed, properly belonged to other Courts differently constituted.[99]

Although lacking a reported opinion, the argument in *Serva* in "the court of all the judges" and the trial which preceded it are reported more or less verbatim. [100] Hewson's preface to the report begins: "It is much to be regretted that no judgment should be delivered in Crown cases" and describes the eleven to two decision invalidating the convictions thus:

> All that can be stated authoritatively respecting the decision is, that the prisoners have been held not to be within the jurisdiction of this country. It is believed, moreover, that the Judges have been of opinion that the Felicidade was unlawfully captured, and on the ground (perhaps amongst others [)] that she had not, and had not had slaves on board.[101]

Lord Chief Justice Denman, however, made a brief statement in dissent: 'It appeared to me that the posses-

---

[99] Arnould, Vol. 2, 442–443.

[100] R. B. Hewson, *The Case of the Queen Against Serva and Others, inclusive of the Trial, and the Argument before the Judges* (London: William Benning & Co. 1846). Hewson is described as a barrister of the Inner Temple. The case is also reported in 1 Dennison's *Crown Cases* 104 and 2 Car. & K. 52 but not to the same degree.

[101] Hewson, ix. In his discussion of *Serva* in *R. v. Keyn,* 2 Ex.D 63 (1876), Lord Chief Justice Cockburn appears to confuse the *Echo* with the *Felicadade.* A different departure from the facts of *Serva* appears in Glanville Williams, "Venue and the Ambit of Criminal Law, Part I", 81 L.Q.R. 276, 287 (1965). There Professor Williams correctly ascribes the outcome of the case to the wrongful seizure of the *Felicidade,* but misdescribes the illegality thus: "...British officers boarded a Brazilian vessel, the *Felicidade,* suspecting her to be engaged in the slave trade. The suspicion turned out to be unfounded..." As noted, the captain of the *Felicidade* testified at trial that the ship was on the way to picking up a cargo of slaves.

sion of the Brazilian vessel by the British officers was a lawful possession, under a seizure made by them of the said ship while employed by Brazilian subjects in the slave trade…" and, in a letter to his Naval son, Captain Denman, the day after the decision, confirming that the decision was based on the invalidity of the capture of the *Felicidade,* characterized the views of the other eleven judges as "the poorest of quibbles."[102] The prisoners were released.

Although its significance in *Serva* arose from the construction of the tangled and incomplete treaty arrangements between Great Britain, Portugal and Brazil[103] and in the *Butterfly* from statutory interpretation, Hewson's observation that the *ratio decedendi* in the *Felicidade* was that the vessel "had not, and had not had slaves on board" applies equally to the *Butterfly*, and it is interesting that both Lord Denman and Howard use the word "quibble" or a more pejorative synonym to disapprove reliance on that circumstance as dispositive in those two cases. However, that eleven out of thirteen British judges took the same view as Judge Betts did on a parallel legal issue and relatively contemporaneously, freeing seven slave traders who had murdered ten British sailors, does undermine Howard's assertion that Judge

---

[102] Arnould, Vol. 2, 202, 204. Lord Denman's attitude may be contrasted with the expressions of outrage at the initiation of the prosecution and the conduct and outcome of the trial, coupled with gratitude for the conclusion of the eleven judges on the appeal, in the anonymous note, "The Brazilian Slave Traders", *The Law Magazine: or Quarterly Review of Jurisprudence,* Vol. IV.,Vol. 35 of the Old Series (1846), 251, 263: "…[E]qually great will be the satisfaction of every lover of liberty and law, that so inauspicious a beginning has had so happy a result… . The happy result of their [the thirteen judges] deliberation has been the discharge of the prisoners from an unjust sentence, the vindication of the laws of England from an incipient reproach, and the maintenance of their world-wide reputation."

[103] See N. 8, *supra.*

Betts's initial decision in the *Morris* case was a disreputable manipulation of the legal process in support of Southern slavery, and his accusation that Judge Betts "could lean over backward to ignore what was obvious to anyone with a less prejudiced mind."[104]

"The Stupidity of Judge Betts's Reasoning"

The point of division between the opinions of Judge Betts in the district court and Justice Thompson in the circuit court in the *Catharine* is illustrated by the language quoted from the latter's opinion at page 76: Judge Betts's analysis segmented the voyage of the vessel into two separate parts, Havana to Africa and Africa to Havana, with only the first part under the American flag, finding no evidence that the object of the *Catharine's* voyage was "continuous and identical", while Justice Thompson's opinion treated both segments as a "one continuous enterprise." Of course Justice Thompson was quite right on the facts, strengthened by the discovery of the 350 pairs of manacles in the hold after the case had reached the circuit court; had the Government put before Judge Betts the evidence which was available to it but apparently never made part of the record in the district court—for example, that Thrasher was a youngster employed by Tyng, a shipbroker specializing in slave ships, or that Pedro Martinez and Simon Perez de Teran, the initial purchaser who defaulted and the final purchaser, were partners together in the largest slave trade establishment in Havana—it seems doubtful that Judge Betts would have come out as he did. But the treatment of a vessel's travels to more than one port as a

---

[104] Howard, 161.

single "continuous voyage" versus treating each segment as a separate voyage was often highly contentious and by no means novel in 1840.

It was one of the major points of friction leading to the War of 1812 between the United States and Great Britain. Initially in *The Polly* in 1800,[105] Sir William Scott, the legendary judge of the Court of Admiralty in London, fashioned a doctrinal work-around for neutral ships to the interdiction of direct trade between a belligerent and its colonies: it treated as two separate voyages, rather than as a single "continuous" one, a voyage carrying cargo from a belligerent colony to the United States and then from the United States to the belligerent's home territory, provided the cargo had been offloaded and passed through Customs in the United States. However, in *The Essex* (1805), affirming the Vice-Admiralty Court in Nassau, the Lords Commissioners of Appeals for admiralty cases in London dismissed factors of the sort relied on in Scott's earlier opinion in the *Polly* as an insufficient basis, as the court below had put it, to grant "to a fraudulently circuitous voyage, those immunities which are withheld from a direct one."[106] The *Essex* decision unleashed a tirade of denunciations from the United States, Henry Adams characterizing it later as judicial "piracy", and exacerbated an existing pamphlet war.[107] Betts, a lawyer who served a term in the House of Representatives starting the year the war ended, can hardly have been ignorant of this dispute.

---

105 *The Polly, Lasky Master*, 2 Rob. 361 (1800).

106 John D. Gordan, III, "Publishing Robinson's *Reports of Cases Argued and Determined in the High Court of Admiralty*", 32 (2014) *Law and History Review,* 525, 560–561; Bradford Perkins, "Sir William Scott and the *Essex,*" *William and Mary Quarterly, Third Ser.,* 13 (1956) 169–183. See also *The William, Tefry*, 5 Rob. 385 (1806).

107 Gordan, 560 n.104.

Years later, Judge Betts was confronted with the same "continuous voyage" issue as had arisen before the War of 1812 and in the *Catharine*, this time while he was adjudicating prize cases arising out of the capture of British vessels carrying cargos ultimately destined for blockaded Southern ports but seized by the United States Navy en route from Europe to Nassau. Whether Justice Thompson's analysis in the *Catharine* two decades earlier was in Judge Betts's mind or not, he used much the same language and segmented nothing, sustaining U.S. Navy seizures of neutral (i.e., British) vessels traveling between neutral ports (i.e. between a British home port and Nassau) if carrying contraband demonstrably intended for future delivery through the blockade to a Confederate port.

For example, the *Springbok* concerned a vessel seized in February 1863 while making for the harbor in Nassau on a voyage documented solely as one from London to Nassau with bills of lading which gave little indication of what the cargo was. Its papers were entirely in order. When the vessel was unloaded on Judge Betts's orders after reaching New York for forfeiture proceedings in the Prize Court, the cargo was found to include army blankets, cavalry sabers and boots, gunpowder, bayonets, 80,000 Confederate army uniform buttons, and 50,000 uniform buttons with "C.S.N." stamped on them. Relying heavily on decisions by Sir William Scott and the Lords Commissioners of Appeals in admiralty cases, Judge Betts held:

> It is well settled that, from the moment a vessel, having on board contraband articles which have a destination to a port of the enemy, leaves her port of departure, she may be legally captured; that it is not necessary to wait until the goods are actually endeavoring to enter the enemy's port; and that, the transpor-

> tation being illegal at its commencement, the penalty immediately attaches.

Judge Betts also held that, given that Nassau was not the ultimate destination of these goods, and that they were intended for transshipment to a blockade runner for delivery to a blockaded port. He quoted Sir William Scott: "'It is a clear and settled principle, that the mere transshipment of a cargo at an intermediate port will not break the continuity of the voyage…'" [108]

In the *Catharine*, of course, there were no slaves on board while the contraband was on the *Springbok*. But what made it contraband was its ultimate destination at a blockaded Confederate port, which was not its immediate destination when seized. Similarly, although the slaves were not yet aboard the *Catharine* when seized, the vessel had been equipped to take them aboard and convey them to their destination and was on its way to do so. In each case the court sustained the seizure by an analysis which embraced the whole of the intended voyage, rather than in segmenting it port by port. The Supreme Court, in an opinion by Chief Justice Chase, affirmed Judge Betts's decision to forfeit the contraband, holding that, as to the cargo, the voyage from London to a blockaded Confederate port was "both in law and in the intent of the parties, one voyage…".[109]

Just as Judge Betts's failure to apply the "continuous voyage" concept in the *Catharine* subjected his decision to reversal by Justice Thompson and criticism for his

---

[108] The *Springbok*, 22 F. Cas. 994, 1007 (Case No. 13,264)(S.D.N.Y. 1863).

[109] 72 U.S. 1, 27 (1867). The Supreme Court held, however, that the proof was insufficient that the owners of the *Springbok* were knowing participants in the contraband character of the cargo, and that although legally detained to seize the contraband, the vessel itself should not have been forfeited.

"stupidity" by Howard, his subsequent application of that doctrine in the *Springbok* brought down upon him denunciation in Parliament and decades of obloquy by foreign academic writers.

In the House of Commons, Judge Betts's decision was denounced as involving "three important and flagrant violations of international law", the third being "the seizure and illegal confiscation of neutral property, under a neutral flag, between two neutral ports, under the pretext that the cargo had an ultimate destination to a belligerent port." The Attorney General's efforts to support Judge Betts in the debate with a different precedent of Sir William Scott's and the argument that Great Britain must not deny "those principles of law which were built up and established by ourselves during the French war" were met by a second member with a sneer at Judge Betts—"that great authority"—for a "doctrine, for which no valid reasons were given" under which "the Federal cruisers might seize vessels going from Liverpool to Scotland...". To this he coupled a denunciation of the federal judiciary and the elderly Prime Minister, Lord Palmerston:

> Moreover, Federal Judges were not like English Judges. ...These inferior Judges might have a bias, therefore, to the prejudice of British subjects, and with regard to their decisions Her Majesty's Government might make some further representations. He felt compelled to make these observations, because unless some pressure was put upon the noble Lord, the Prime Minister, no justice would be done to British subjects. The noble Lord was a brave man against a feeble adversary. If he had to face a Greek or a Neapolitan his courage was enormous—he would execute severe reprisals against Brazil; he would levy war upon the defenseless Chinese or Japanese; but the moment he was in front of an antagonist whose physical or moral strength was in the least degree formidable, he shrank

> from the contest, and left the injured British subject to obtain his remedy as best he could. ... [W]hen he had to meet "the great Abraham," "he bent low, and in a bondman's key, with bated breath and whispering humbleness," said, "Fair Sir, you spit on me on Wednesday last; you spurned me such a day, and for these courtesies I now obey your bidding."[110]

Similarly, a British barrister specializing in international law began his paper on "Judge Betts and Prize Law" by characterizing him as "a political judge, swayed in his judicial action by political considerations" and his "judicial qualities" as "sinister." In addressing the decision in the *Springbok,* he summed up against the doctrine of continuous voyage by asserting that "[t]he doctrine evolved exclusively on the Civil War cases: and they in turn were inspired by Judge Betts."[111] Academics in England and Europe said much the same thing: "'The American decisions have been universally reprobated outside the United States, and would probably now find no defenders in their own country.'"[112]

On the other hand, American commentators insisted that Judge Betts's application of the doctrine of continuous voyage to the cargo in the *Springbok* was in harmony with

---

[110] *Hansard's Parliamentary Debates,* CLXXIII, 501–524 (February 12, 1864).

[111] Thomas Baty, "Judge Betts and Prize Law", 11 (1925) *Transactions of the Grotius Society,* 21, 23. Although the colloquy reported following the text of the article suggests substantial disagreement on the part of others, the author remained unconvinced. Thomas Baty, "The History of Continuous Voyage," 90 (1941) U. Penn. L. Rev. 127. See also Vaughan Lowe, "The Place of Dr. Thomas Baty in the International Law Studies of the 20th Century," (Oxford Faculty of Law Legal Studies Research Working Paper No 11/2008, March 2008).

[112] Hall, *International Law* (1895), 694 n., quoted in J. Dundas White, *The Seizure of the* Bundesrath, 17 L.Q.R. 12, 22–23 (1901).

precedent and correctly decided.[113] Moreover, ironically but not surprisingly, once Great Britain became a belligerent in World War I, its Prize Court adopted Judge Betts's jurisprudence enthusiastically;

> ...[F]ollowing the precedents set by the Prize Courts of the United States during the Civil War... [t]he Prize Courts, both of Great Britain and of the other belligerent States, extended the doctrine of Continuous Voyage beyond the application which it had hitherto received. But this extension was in conformity with the line of development of the law. The decisions of the Prize Courts of the United States during the Civil War marked an important stage in the movement....[114]

Given the controversial nature of the doctrine of continuous voyage since the *Essex* decision in 1805 and the continuing bitter disagreement in the profession about its scope, Howard goes too far in suggesting that Judge Betts, denounced for applying it in the Civil War prize cases despite the expanded powers of a belligerent recognized by international law and with the support of the Supreme Court of the United States, was "stupid" and *ipso facto* pro-slavery when he did not apply it in the *Catharine*, twenty years earlier, in the absence of a war or a treaty.

---

[113] Charles Burke Elliott, "The Doctrine of Continuous Voyages", 1 (1907) *American Journal of International Law*, 61, 82–104; James Bassett Moore, *A Digest of International Law* (Washington, D.C., Gov't. Printing Office, 1906), Vol. 7, Section 1261; Randolph Greenfield Adams, "Growth of Belligerent Rights Over Neutral Trade", 68 (1920) U. Penn. L. Rev. 20.

[114] C. John Colombos, *A Treatise on the Law of Prize* (London: Sweet & Maxwell 1926), xiii–xiv.

APPENDIX

The First Day of the Trial of Isaac Morris

Decision of Judge Samuel Rossiter Betts in the *Butterfly*

The First Day of the Trial of Isaac Morris

"United States Circuit Court.
"Present – Judges Thompson and Betts.

"Nov. 30.— The United States versus Isaac P. Morris, indicted for a violation of the Slave Act, passed 10th May, 1800.— The District Attorney briefly opened the case on the part of the Government, and cited the law which he intended to rely on for a conviction, if the facts should be made out to the satisfaction of the jury. The learned gentleman also made some severe remarks on the prostitution of the American flag to the nefarious purpose of carrying on the Slave Trade.

"Mr. Hamilton said, that before the examination of the first witness was commenced, he wished to ascertain which count in the indictment they meant to proceed on. The first count charged the accused with serving on board an American vessel, called the '*Butterfly*,' and the second charged him with serving, at the same period of time, on board the schooner '*Butterfly*,' a foreign vessel. The learned gentleman contended that his client could not be serving on board of two vessels at the same time.

"The Court said, that if the indictment charged the defendant with being on board two distinct vessels, it might have some force; but as it was a mere question of ownership, the Court thought the defendants could not compel the prosecution to make any election.

"Robert Thomas examined.— I am an officer in Her Britannic Majesty's service, as master's assistant to the "Dolphin," commanded by Lieutenant Holland. That vessel has recently been employed in the suppression of the Slave Trade, on the Coast of Africa. In the month of September, I was at Sierra Leone, and saw the schooner '*Butterfly*' brought in; that same vessel now lies in the harbor of New York. She was captured on suspicion of Slaving, and in the belief that she was Spanish property. The prisoner was on board at the time, and, at a subsequent period, she was placed in my charge to come to New York.

"The District Attorney was proceeding to inquire of the witness respecting the fittings of the '*Butterfly*,' when Mr. Hamilton, jun., objected to any testimony on that point, because the search was not made by competent authority but without the least shadow of right on the part of the captors.

"The District Attorney having replied, his Honour, Judge Thompson, delivered the opinion of the Court. His Honour said the Court did not deem the question of the right of seizure by a British Cruiser to have anything to do with the matter before the jury. Neither did the cases which had been cited apply to this case; they were vessels claimed by the captors, and not prosecutions for the infraction of a penal statute. It was of no import how the United States came by the proof, and could not be permitted to interfere with the enforcement of the law. It was a question between the two Governments, and not to be mooted here. The Court, therefore, overruled the objection, and directed the District Attorney to proceed.

"Examination resumed.— The vessel had twenty-four large leaguers, each capable of holding from two hundred and fifty to three hundred gallons of water. Six of these casks for holding water were made up, and eighteen of them called shooks were in the hold. Two such casks would be sufficient for an ordinary crew on board such a vessel as the '*Butterfly*'. Vessels employed in the Slave Trade are fitted up with such conveniences for carrying water for the negroes.

"The '*Butterfly*' had also a quantity of timber ready to fit in for a slave-deck. The timber and planks were all found on board, and marked with red chalk, as if by a carpenter, to show where they fitted together. A carpenter could have put the deck up in one day. Slave coppers were also on board, similar to what have been found on board of

Slave-ships for the purpose of cooking for the negroes.

"The cargo was next proved from the bills of lading, which the witness identified, together with the two logs, and other ships' documents. The papers, books, &c, the witness said he had received from the commander of the 'Dolphin.' Such cargoes as are on board the '*Butterfly*' are commonly carried to the coast of Africa by vessels engaged in the Slave Trade.

"District Attorney.— Did Morris say anything to you about his capacity on board the '*Butterfly*'?"

"Witness. — He admitted that he was master.

"The District Attorney produced the register, dated at New Orleans, and endorsed on the back that 'Nathan Farnsworth had assigned the command of the '*Butterfly*' to Isaac P. Morris, in the presence of the Consul of the United States at Havana.' Signed "J.A. Smith, Vice-Consul."

"Cross-examined.—The vessel was not in her direct route to the Island of Principe when captured. I understood she was going to St. Paul's for water. The casks found on board were peculiar for the Slave Trade, and if I saw them in a cooper's shop I should say they were for that traffic. The planks were stowed on the side of the vessel, and not below the cargo. I believe there were more than twenty persons on board at the time of the capture. Palm-oil is one of the principal articles of export from the coast of Africa. A vessel in an honest pursuit would carry a cargo similar to that on board the '*Butterfly.*' A Portuguese pen[n]ant is on board the '*Butterfly*', 'but it was never hoisted while I was on board. I had occasion to speak a vessel, and then I hoisted the American ensign. I tied the flag in a knot, which I deemed a signal for a boat to come on board. "

By Mr. Cutting.— I have never seen any slaves or negroes on board the '*Butterfly.*' I have no knowledge of that vessel having been actually engaged in the transportation of slaves from one port to another.

"George Darling examined.— I was one of the crew of the 'Dolphin,' and was on board when she captured the '*Butterfly*' off Cape St. Paul, on the coast of Africa. The prisoner was on board of the schooner and said he was the master. I do not know how ma[n]y persons were on board. He was the only American; the others were Spaniards.

"This witness gave a similar account of the cargo to that testified to by Mr. Thomas.

"Cross-examined.— The '*Butterfly'* did not attempt to escape from the 'Dolphin.' We fired a shot and she hove-to immediately. The papers were not asked for until next morning, and the prisoner gave up the papers immediately. The prisoner was overhauled, and so was the supercargo, and some doubloons found on him. The passengers and crew were landed at Quittah, and their clothes and necessaries given up to them. I saw no slaves or negroes on board. If there had been any slaves the cargo would have been out. Every man requires three pints of water on that coast per day. The usual watering places are St. Paul's and Quittah, though in our service we go to Principe.

"Here the prosecution rested.

"The Defendant's counsel called one witness, and he only was asked if Farnsworth was an American citizen.

"Mr. Hamilton, jun., made his maiden speech in the case, on the part of the defendant, and cited the following case :—

"*'The case of the brig* 'Alexandra,' 3d *Mason's Reports, page* 175; *libelled and seized, on the Act of April,* 1818, *March,* 1794, and *May*, 1800.'—At the trial the only count which was sustained by the evidence, was founded on the first section of the Act of 1800, ch.51. Upon the evidence, Blair, for the claimant, contended that there was no offence within the Act, even supposing the vessel was engaged in the Slave Trade, because no slaves had been taken on board, or were on board during the voyage for transportation, which was necessary to bring the case within the Act.

"Blake, District Attorney, contended that the employment in the Slave Trade was the thing prohibited by the Act, and slaves were not necessary to be taken on board to complete the offence. He cited the '*Plattsburg*,' before Judge Van Ness, at New York, and the '*Fortune*': (1 Dodson, 81.)

"Judge Storey [sic] said— 'The first section of the Act of 1800, c.51, on which alone this prosecution can be maintained, declares that it shall be unlawful for any citizen, &c, directly or indirectly, to hold or have any right on property in any vessel *employed, or made use* of in the transportation or carrying of slaves from, &c, under penalty of forfeiture. The question is, whether the penalty is affixed to the mere employment of the vessel, for the business and for the purpose of transporting slaves, or whether transportation is necessary. My opinion is, that the former is the true construction of the Act. We often speak of vessels employed in the coasting-trade and fisheries, and the Acts of Congress use the same language when actual transportation and actual fishing are not intended, but the purpose and business of the voyage are the coasting-trade and fisheries. And it has never been doubted that a vessel licensed for the coasting-trade and fisheries, and on a voyage for that purpose, was truly employed in such trade or fisheries, although no goods were in the course of actual transportation, and no fisheries had been yet attempted.

"'Let us look, then, to the claims of these statutes.' Here the judge recited the Acts, and went on to say 'that as every vessel fitted out for the purpose of the Slave Trade may be truly and accurately said to be employed in that business, and carrying it on as soon as she has sailed on the voyage, it matters not at what point of the voyage she is captured; her enterprise is the Slave Trade, and every act done on such a voyage is an act of carrying it on. In the case of the '*Fortune*' (1 Dodson, 81–86,) Sir William Scott held a similar opinion. I, therefore, interpret the language of the first section by the language of the third and fourth, and I think that the legislature intended the same thing in all, and that is, that the employment in the business, and for the purposes of the Slave Trade, and not merely the actual transportation of slaves, should be prohibited and punished.'

"Decree of condemnation affirmed."

"The learned gentleman said, that notwithstanding this decision of Judge Story, it ought to be reversed, as the first section of the Act should be consonant with the second and third sections of the same, which contemplated a full consummation of the offence, and which consummation should consist, in order to satisfy the words of the section, [of] the actual receiving on board of slaves in order to constitute the carrying of slaves. He contended, also, that the Slave Trade had been protected by the constitution, and up to the year 1808, slaves had been introduced into this country from the coast of Africa.

"Mr. Butler sustained the views of Judge Story, and contended that the offence was complete if the vessel was fitted out to carry slaves.

"Mr. Cutting supported the opinions of Mr. Hamilton.

"The Court said that though they might differ in their views from Judge Story, yet comity required that, as they were circuit judges, of equal jurisdiction, their opinions should not clash; and it was therefore important that the true construction of these laws should be understood throughout the several States; and, in this view, the Court had concluded to decide in the present case, and to send their opinion to the Supreme Court of the United States for its ultimate adjudication.

"It was then agreed by the Counsel on both sides that it was difficult to procure the attendance of the foreign witnesses; that their testimony, in case the decision of Judge Story should be sustained by the Supreme Court, should be used on the future trial of the present case, and that the jury be discharged without a verdict, and the prisoner remanded; also that the case of Peterson take the same course.

"The Court then adjourned."

Decision of Judge Samuel Rossiter Betts in the Butterfly

In Admiralty.
"The United States v. the Schooner "Butterfly."

The libel demands the condemnation of this vessel as being employed in the Slave Trade in contravention of the Act of Congress of May 10, 1800.

The construction given this Statute, at the late term of the Supreme Court in reference to this very case, leaves it now for this Court only to ascertain two facts. First, was this schooner on a slaving voyage when arrested, and if so, secondly, whether the slaves were to be transported from one foreign country or place to another. There being no direct and positive testimony to these points, t[he] inquiries are to be answered by weighing the inferences and presumptions justly arising from the facts and circumstances in proof.

It is to be assumed, on entering upon the subject, that it is lawful for an American vessel to trade to the Coast of Africa, and to carry for such purposes all the articles found on board this schooner, and also that every article of her lading was proper for and adapted to a lawful trade there; for although there is no particular evidence that the large boiler, or the bundles of shooks, or the loose lumber found on board this vessel could be advantageously disposed of on the coast, or had any of them been before used in the trade there, yet without express testimony to the contrary the presumption would be in favour of their being proper articles for that market, or if they possessed no known value there at least, they might be carried, and offered in such trade without subjecting the vessel to any injurious imputation. Considering, then, that all the lading of this vessel might be lawfully employed in trade on that coast, and that she was directed to districts where an innocent commerce may be carried on, it will not be sufficient for the prosecution to show that these facts are equally compatible with an engagement in the illicit trade denounced by the Act of Congress. Such a state of the case would entitle the claimant to an acquittal of the vessel; for the United States must show by preponderating evidence that the vessel had violated the Act, and when the testimony as well applies to an innocent as an illicit enterprize, the law will not regard it as creating a presumption of guilt. But it must be taken into the account that an acquittal would not be pronounced because of the failure to bring any proof against the vessel, but because the facts which may properly be received as importing the purpose charged against her are placed in equilibrium by the consideration that they are alike consistent with her being employed in an honest adventure.

The additional facts and circumstances then are not to be weighed as if alone, and all the evidence produced against the vessel, but they are to be sifted and applied to this equivocal or ambiguous posture of the case, that it may then be determined whether such equilibrium is disturbed by the addition of these particulars, and if so, to which side their weight preponderates. The most prominent of these particulars are the change of the Master and crew of the vessel at Havana, the description of the new crew, and the additional number put on board as passengers, and the mode and terms under which the vessel was employed. The vessel appears to have sailed from New Orleans with an American crew, and with her Owner as Master; at Havana all this crew was discharged, and the First Mate became Master in place of the Owner. A new crew of Spaniards and Portuguese were shipped: no reason is indicated for this entire change of the command and equipage of the vessel. She is then chartered to a Spanish house in Havana to carry a cargo to the Isles Principe, St. Thome, or to the north coast of Africa, with an allowance of 20 days for unloading the cargo and 20 dollars per day demurrage beyond that period; and it is proved that she, in capacity and build, corresponds with vessels employed in transporting slaves, and is not well adapted to carrying freight. It is in proof that the ship's company could unload the cargo, and with the aid of a carpenter, construct 18 water-tanks out of the shooks in bundles, and lay a false deck with the lumber on board, within a period of 10 or 14 days, and accordingly the term of 30 days reserved in the Charter-party could not be necessary for the delivery of the cargo, and must have been introduced with a view to some other consideration; and because this delay was wholly unnecessary for the vessel, the presumption would be direct and strong that it must be one connected with the disposition of the cargo of the Owner; and this inference is perhaps to be regarded as conclusive with the aid of the additional fact that no return cargo is stipulated, and therefore there could be no interest to the ship owner to prolong the voyage. It is in proof that the places designated in the Charter-party are those to which vessels resort for the purchase of slaves with the barter or proceeds of her cargo until enough are obtained to complete her lading. The Charterer had the further privilege of detaining the vessel *ad libitum* after the expiration of 30 days on paying 20 dollars per day demurrage without any stipulation to supply return freights; and it is to be observed, that the current of freight on the outward voyage (including the 30 days' detention), would be nearly 40 dollars per day according to the ordinary duration of such voyages, and that accordingly the owner leaves his vessel to the control of the charterer in that dangerous climate for an indefinite period of time, at a rate of compensation far short of what was paid her on the run. Demurrage is regarded as an extended freight. (Holt, Shipping, 325); and to be stipulated between the parties with a view to the actual earnings on the voyage (*ibid.* 338), and is so awarded by a Court and Jury when the rate is not expressed in the

Charter-party (Holt, 338).

The Court must notice judicially the fact that Havana is a port engaged actively in the trade of slaves transported from the coast of Africa. Upon the points under review then the evidence assumes this aspect:— a vessel of the kind, usually employed in the Slave Trade, supplied with such cargo as is commonly used in purchasing slaves, and with fitments adapting her to their transportation, sails from Havana to the coast of Africa for an agreed freight out, but to remain at the disposal of the charterer on the coast without any stipulation for return cargo, and for a period of time free of demurrage not shown to be usual or in any way necessary merely for the delivery of her cargo, and to continue at his further disposal without limitation of time on a rate of compensation less than the earnings of the outward voyage. The next additional class of facts relates to the composition of the ship's company. The crew consisted of eight mariners, all Portuguese and Spaniards, the Master being the only American on board. In addition to these were the charterer, a Spaniard, and 14 other persons, represented to be passengers, who, as appears by the list of "passengers" found on board the brig, "were to be landed in port or the coast as the Master or Consignee may direct."

Twelve of these were Spaniards, one Portuguese, one from Minorca, and one from the Canaries, but all residents of Havana. On examining the passports furnished these individuals at Havana for the voyage, they are (with but one or two excepted) described as *mariners*. The proof is, that this vessel could supply water and accommodations for from 250 to 300 slaves, and that a larger crew would be requisite to secure and manage a vessel loaded with slaves than would be necessary to navigate her on an ordinary voyage.

There is no proof that any passage-money was charged or received for carrying out this number of persons; nor is any reason assigned for their being taken from their place of residence and left at the discretion of the Master or Consignee in the midst of a savage population, without any stipulation for their sustenance there or return home.

These facts unexplained supply a vehement presumption that such persons were to be continued with the vessel, and were connected with her enterprise.

With these considerations is to be combined the manner in which the adventure was arranged and set on foot, as supplying indicia of the objects in view between the parties at the time. The vessel retained her American papers; and it would certainly present a case for surprise and inquiry if she was destined on an ordinary trading voyage, that all her men should be discharged, and she placed in the possession of a Mate only to protect the interests of her Owner whilst she took onboard 23 others, all foreigners, and whose language it does not appear he understood at all. Such a proceeding may be consistent with the most perfect integrity of purpose, but the departure from the precaution and prudence commonly exercised by owners of vessels is so flagrant as to demand some explanation by proof of the motives and occasion justifying it.

The charterer, as a Spaniard, must be held to know that the vessel laden with the articles he was to put on board would, if Spanish property, be subject to capture under the Treaty with Great Britain of June 28, 1835; and the owner is also, in judgment of law, cognizant of the laws of the port with or from which the vessel is to trade.

It is to be regarded then, as a fact brought home to the notice of the owner and the charterer, that the evidence supplied by the loading of this vessel would be complete proof under the laws of Spain that she was employed in the Slave Trade, and if found approaching the Coasts of Africa so laden she would be subject to condemnation as a slave trader. An innocent trade between Havana and

Africa is equally permitted to Spanish vessels as to American: but, as matters of evidence, the Court must notice that the parties were arranging this voyage with a full knowledge that the facts exhibited on board would be full proof in a Spanish Court, with respect to a Spanish vessel, that the adventure was not lawful, but contemplated a traffic in slaves. This consequence is avoided to the charterer only by securing the guarantee of the American flag; and the inference that the flag is used to protect Spanish property and Spaniards from the operation of their own Treaty would be so direct and forcible, as matters of evidence, as to impose on those acting under knowledge of all these particulars the necessity of explaining away by competent and credible proofs their bearing and import. The question to be tried under the Act of Congress is precisely that which would have been presented under the Spanish Treaty, had these parties rendered the vessel Spanish property, and that is, whether in this adventure she was employed in the Slave Trade. In determining this question according to the rules of our own law, it is by no means inadmissible evidence, or as an item of presumptive proof of slight weight, to show that the parties acted under knowledge that the same adventure in a Spanish vessel would be regarded a slaving voyage. It would afford *prima facie* evidence that the American flag was used to screen facts from examination whilst the understanding of all parties where the transaction was had unequivocally proved that this vessel was so employed.

The French Treaty with Great Britain contains precisely the same provisions in this behalf as that with Spain; and it is clear upon the proofs that it was notorious on all the coast to which this voyage was directed, that a vessel so fitted out as she was would be regarded as engaged in the Slave Trade; and the owner must, under the circumstances, be chargeable with knowledge of the interpretation and import of these circumstances in reference to such an undertaking, and they ought therefore to be understood in that sense as against him, unless he offers testimony demonstrating that in this particular case such inference is not true. *Prima facie* evidence, in the absence of exculpatory proofs, will justify the condemnation of property seized (7 Cranch, 748); and the party claiming property is always bound to obviate such evidence by offering explanatory proofs on his side.

I am constrained, under this view of the various circumstances connected with the case, to declare that there is strong *prima facie* proof that this vessel was, when arrested, employed in the Slave Trade.

The remaining inquiry is, whether the evidence also proves that she was employed in the transportation of slaves from one foreign country to another. The argument for the claimant is, that the vessel being American, the presumption, in the absence of direct proof to the contrary, is that she was destined to the United States, and that a transportation of slaves from Africa to this country is not interdicted by the Act of 1800. But it is to be remarked that the inquiry in hand is not necessarily to be solved by positive testimony alone; it may as well be ascertained by an inquiry into collateral and concomitant facts and circumstances as any other particular connected with the adventure. Proceeding upon this investigation with the fact already ascertained, that the vessel was to transport slaves from Africa, we have these particulars to guide us in determining their destination.

The crew are residents of Havannah, and, with the exception of the Master, foreigners to this country, and not speaking our language; and the cargo and crew being entirely from that port, the inference would be a reasonable one that the vessel was to return to the same place, unless there is some stipulation shown that the voyage should end elsewhere.

The shipping articles state that the vessel is bound from Havana to the Isles of Principe, St. Thome, or any other port on the North Coast of Africa; the voyage not to exceed twelve months.

This being a slaving voyage that may continue twelve months, the presumption is forcible and irresistible that it was not to terminate in Africa, and with leaving the crew in that barbarous region; and as the place of ulterior destination is concealed upon the articles, the inference is direct and strong that the vessel was to return to the place of her departure, and where the ship's company belonged.

This is again strengthened by the import of the Charter-party. The charterer, who was with the vessel, had the control of her, under the name of demurrage, for the whole period of the crew's service, if he chose to occupy her on the coast; and no return freight being stipulated, and no privilege to the Master reserved of securing freight from any other quarter, the presumption is most violent that she was to be laden and sailed under the directions of the charterer. He, it appears, was a resident merchant at Havana, and the conclusion would be equally direct and satisfactory that he was to bring back the proceeds of his cargo to his home port.

The results are arrived at, it is true, by inferences and presumptions, but it appears to me they necessarily flow from the facts and circumstances brought to view by the evidence in this case.

Circumstances which by themselves, or in one connexion, may be unimportant or importing nothing suspicious may by a different relation and association become pregnant with significant accusation. It is such association of facts and circumstances which composes what the law denominates circumstantial evidence, a description of proof equally conclusive upon courts and juries as the most positive and direct testimony; it therefore in no way evades the relevancy and effect of the particulars here renewed towards establishing the conclusion to which they so forcibly conduce to show that in a different state of things they would be regarded as of no moment. This vessel might have been directed to the north of Europe under all these concomitant circumstances without the facts conducing to prove she was engaged in a slave voyage; the purpose and object of an adventure always taking their complexion from the ends manifestly in view. We so judge in questions of contraband and smuggling, and in administering the law of crimes and punishments, a class of particulars in one connexion, innocent in another, become swift witnesses of condemnation.

It is only to be further remarked that this vessel and her employment being placed in a position of apparent criminality her Owner was called upon to clear her from the imputation by furnishing proof that her employment was legal and innocent.

This, if the fact was so, he would be enabled to do by the testimony of her Master and crew. Not having presented any evidence on his part the case is to be determined upon the consideration only of that which has been brought to bear against the integrity and lawfulness of her adventure.

Upon a careful consideration of the case, I am of opinion that it is satisfactorily proved that the "*Butterfly,*" at the time of her arrest, was employed in the transportation or carrying of slaves from one foreign place to another within the meaning of the Act of Congress of May 10, 1800, as expounded by the Supreme Court, and accordingly I pronounce a decree of condemnation against her, her tackle, apparel, &c, together with costs of suit.

I, Frederick J. Betts, Clerk of the District Court of the United States, for the district of New York, do hereby certify the foregoing to be a true copy of the original decision now remaining on file in my office.

New York, April 13, 1840

INDEX

www.ingramcontent.com/pod-product-compliance
Ingram Content Group UK Ltd.
Pitfield, Milton Keynes, MK11 3LW, UK
UKHW041840031026
15587UKWH00002B/909

9 781616 195458